Praise for *Go Mobile*

"A thorough introduction to the next frontier for permission marketing: mobile."

—**Seth Godin,** author of *We Are All Weird*
and *Permission Marketing*

"Mobile marketing is a huge challenge for companies to consider. Learn all you can through books like this, and through diving in yourself."

—**Chris Brogan,** president of Human Business Works
and coauthor of *Trust Agents*

"*Go Mobile* is your must-read road map to the widely traveled road of mobile users. If you want to excel past a basic understanding of mobile marketing and truly connect with on-the-go consumers, study this book!"

—**Michael Stelzner,** founder of Social Media Examiner
and author of *Launch*

"Mobile is leading the post-PC era of consumer engagement. Without defining a mobile experience, you're missing an opportunity to connect your business to the future of consumerism."

—**Brian Solis,** author of *The End of Business as Usual*
and *Engage!*

"*Go Mobile* is an excellent resource to arm advertisers with information about mobile consumer behavior, how companies are tackling the new mobile environment, and ways to jump start their mobile marketing initiatives."

—**Michelle Scruggs,** senior account manager, Google

"This book gets to the core of mobile marketing and will be a valuable, go-to reference whether you are just taking the first steps in mobile marketing, or need to further develop your current mobile marketing strategy."

—**Nancy Costopulos,** chief marketing officer,
American Marketing Association

"Mobile marketing is the next big thing. *Go Mobile* gives you the tools you need to dive right in!"

—**Erik Qualman,** digital leader and best-selling author
of *Socialnomics*

"Must-review material for everyone to keep in control of the mobile revolution before it sweeps you off your feet."

—Anne Holland, publisher, WhichTestWon.com

"Jeanne and Jamie are masters at demystifying the world of mobile marketing and putting thoughts into action. From the very first page you get the idea that anyone can learn to activate this channel—if they know what questions to ask. Fortunately, this book helps them brilliantly with both the questions, and the answers."

—Andy Goldsmith, VP, Creative and Brand Strategy,
American Cancer Society

"With so many consumers depending on mobile technologies but so few businesses taking advantage of what it has to offer, read *Go Mobile* today to be well ahead of the competition—guaranteed!"

—Tamar Weinberg, Techipedia.com

"Not having a mobile marketing strategy today is like not having a website strategy a decade ago. Read this book."

—Dharmesh Shah, Cofounder, HubSpot

"Every marketer who is charged with taking their brand mobile needs to read *Go Mobile*, Hopkins and Turner take the fear out of mobile marketing by supplying simple, actionable items that can be implemented quickly to help take your brand to the next level."

—Drew James, associate publisher,
Target Marketing and Fundraising Success

"Don't think of mobile devices as smaller, mobile PCs, they're something completely different. *Go Mobile* gives you all the tools you need to leverage this new and emerging channel. Better still, Jeanne and Jamie give their advice in an engaging, readable style."

—Malcolm McRoberts, senior vice president,
Deluxe Corporation

GO MOBILE

LOCATION–BASED MARKETING, APPS, MOBILE OPTIMIZED AD CAMPAIGNS, 2D CODES, AND OTHER MOBILE STRATEGIES TO GROW YOUR BUSINESS

JEANNE HOPKINS
JAMIE TURNER

WILEY

John Wiley & Sons, Inc.

Published by John Wiley & Sons, Inc., Hoboken, New Jersey.
Published simultaneously in Canada.

For general information on our other products and services or for technical support, please contact our Customer Care Department within the United States at (800) 762-2974, outside the United States at (317) 572-3993 or fax (317) 572-4002.

Wiley publishes in a variety of print and electronic formats and by print-on-demand. Some material included with standard print versions of this book may not be included in e-books or in print-on-demand. If this book refers to media such as a CD or DVD that is not included in the version you purchased, you may download this material at http://booksupport.wiley.com. For more information about Wiley products, visit www.wiley.com.

Library of Congress Cataloging-in-Publication Data:

Hopkins, Jeanne, 1957-
    Go mobile : location-based marketing, apps, mobile optimized ad campaigns, 2D codes, and other mobile strategies to grow your business / Jeanne Hopkins, Jamie Turner.
        p. cm.
    Includes index.
    ISBN 978-1-118-16778-6 (cloth); ISBN 978-1-118-22640-7 (ebk); ISBN 978-1-118-26428-7 (ebk); ISBN 978-1-118-23954-4 (ebk)
        1. Internet marketing.   2. Mobile commerce.   3. Mobile communication systems.
    I. Turner, Jamie, 1961-   II. Title.
    HF5415.1265.H665   2012
    658.8'72—dc23
                                                                        2011042400

Printed in the United States of America

10 9 8 7 6 5 4 3 2 1

To my parents, Joe and Sarah, who gave me my first library card and instilled in me a love of books, and to my husband, John, and daughters, Julianna and Isabella, who give me the strength and stability to live in this mobile world.

—Jeanne Hopkins

To my wife, Dayna, and my three girls, McKensie, Grace, and Lily. You are all the light of my life. Also dedicated to my sister, Nanci Turner Steveson, an author in her own right, who once said to me, "Get off your arse and write your next book proposal!"

—Jamie Turner

Contents

Foreword

Reaching Your Buyers in Real Time—Wherever They Are

In Tokyo's Roppongi entertainment district, you find several hundred bars within walking distance of the subway station. Yet only a few are visible from the main street; the vast majority are tucked away on the upper floors of back-street buildings. To differentiate, many cater to highly refined customer preferences. So if you want to listen to classic reggae while sipping a Red Stripe, there is a bar for you in Roppongi. But how do you find these establishments when you're thirsty and confused in an unfamiliar city?

Your mobile device of course!

Because buyers use their mobiles to search for products and services *in the time of need* (as I do when I'm in some faraway city), you've got an opportunity to reach them when they are ready to buy. The elapsed time from firing up a mobile app like foursquare or Google Mobile to a customer walking in the door is now measured in minutes (or even seconds).

Adding GPS (global positioning system) capability to mobiles has transformed a once mundane voice-only mobile phone into a targeted weapon focused on proximate surroundings. With onboard GPS capability, the mobile user gains awareness of nearby people, companies, and locations, even in unfamiliar territory like the bar district of Tokyo. When someone is using his or her mobile with geolocation capability, the location of that person is pinpointed. This is truly revolutionary. That's why mobile devices comprise the fastest-growing and most fascinating field in real-time market engagement. That's also why an understanding of mobile marketing is so important.

In my travels, I've noticed more and more executives, as well as reporters and analysts, using mobile devices, especially iPads, to take notes during meetings. I've also seen these important people on the go with their iPhones, BlackBerrys, and the like in constant use. So it's not just people working in local businesses like retail shops and restaurants who need to understand mobile marketing; this is essential information for large organizations, B2B outfits, nonprofits, and educational institutions alike.

The challenge is to understand this new landscape in order to get your business into the mix at that precise moment of decision. There are many ways to reach people via mobile, such as applications like foursquare, SMS messaging, image scanning such as QR codes, and others. You will learn about all of these in this book through fascinating examples of success from organizations large and small.

Also discussed is the often-overlooked but essential requirement that you make your website mobile-friendly. As people use mobile web browsers on their iPhones, Androids, or other devices, displaying your content quickly and optimizing it for viewing on smaller screens is how you drive business. Many sites still don't have a mobile-friendly architecture, and those organizations miss out on opportunities to sell to the many people now accessing their sites from wireless devices. You'll learn about mobile websites in these pages, too.

Perhaps the fastest-growing aspect of mobile marketing is mobile applications. It seems there really is an app for everything these days. For example, the SitOrSquat bathroom-finder application for iPhone and other devices, as of this writing, indexes more than 100,000 public restrooms, all geolocated and rated for cleanliness. Clean bathrooms receive a Sit rating; dirty ones, a Squat. So after a beer or two in that Tokyo bar, you can find an acceptable potty as you stroll back to your hotel. Heck, I've got my own free David Meerman Scott iPhone and iPad applications. My applications deliver my blog posts, Twitter feed, and videos to people in real time, and link to my online bookstore on Amazon.

When I created the New Rules Social Media Book Series with John Wiley & Sons, Inc., I said that it was essential to have a book about mobile marketing. Fortunately, Jeanne Hopkins and Jamie Turner agreed to write *Go Mobile*. Either one of them alone would have written a great book on mobile marketing; having them collaborate doubles the fun. I learned a great deal by reading this book and I'm confident that you will too.

Mobile offers marketers the power to reach buyers at the *exact time and place* they're looking for what you offer. It is a revolutionary tool for building business, and it's easy to learn. Turn the page to find out how.

—David Meerman Scott
Author of *The New Rules of Marketing & PR*, and the
new book *Newsjacking*
www.WebInkNow.com
twitter.com/dmscott

Acknowledgments

Hmmmm. This is interesting. This book is packed with insightful marketing tips and, yet, the first thing you read is the Acknowledgments section. That can only mean one of two things—either you're one of our editors (who are required to read every word of this masterpiece) or you're someone snooping around to see if we remembered to put your name in the book.

Well, we did put your name in the book. But you're going to have to read the entire thing to find out where we put it. It's buried deep inside, so you'll have to read each and every one of the 59,877 words.

Of course, if you want to save some time, you could just read the next few paragraphs (which seems to be where you're headed, right?).

Alrighty, then. Let's get on with the task at hand, which is to acknowledge *you* and all the other people who have helped us write this book. So here goes.

We'd like to thank each and every one of the 6,875,843,985 people living on the planet.

Seriously. We'd like to thank all the people living on the planet. Come to think of it, we'd like to thank all the nonliving people on the planet, too. After all, if we limited our acknowledgments to the names we wrote on the yellow sticky notes plastered on our computer monitors, we'd invariably miss someone since yellow sticky notes have a tendency to drop off monitors and fall behind desks where they collect dust until we find them next year and say, "Oh, darn. We forgot to acknowledge (fill in your name here)."

So, thank you. All 6,875,843,985 of you who are living. (And all the dead folks. Thank you, too!)

Okay, now that we've covered our bases, are you ready for some specific names? Here goes.

In no particular order, we'd like to thank Raphael Rivilla, Nicole Hall, Nanci Turner Steveson, Simms Jenkins, Alan Deeter, Kyle Wegner, Patrick Miller, Mike Turner, Jr., Chuck Smith, Cindy Krum,

Tim Miller, David Meerman Scott, Dan Zarrella, Mike Volpe, Dave Stack, Dharmesh Shah, Brian Halligan, the marketing team at Hub-Spot, the team at BKV, the folks at A School Bell Rings, and Janice Borzendowski.

We'd also very specifically like to thank and acknowledge the folks at John Wiley & Sons, Inc. who helped us craft this book. We really couldn't have done it without your wisdom and guidance. You include Shannon Vargo, Elana Schulman, Lauren Freestone, Kim Dayman, and Heather Condon. Thank you all for your hard work and professionalism!

Finally, we'd both like to acknowledge God's role in our lives. None of this would have been possible without You.

Introduction

Are you curious about how to use mobile marketing to grow your business? Would you like to know how to use Quick Response (QR) codes, mobile apps, location-based marketing, and other mobile tools to increase your sales and revenue? Are you wondering how companies like Coca-Cola, Delta, and Starbucks use mobile marketing to connect with their customers?

If so, we have some good news. Answering those questions is exactly what we've set out to do in *Go Mobile*. We've demystified mobile marketing and repackaged it as a simple, easy-to-understand tool that you can use to grow your sales and revenue. The questions you have about how to set up, launch, and run a mobile marketing campaign we have answer in this book.

It's worth noting that mobile marketing isn't just an *evolutionary* new technology; it's a *revolutionary* new technology. More, it's a once-in-a-generation shift in the way consumers connect with brands. And it's going to have greater impact than radio, TV, and the personal computer—*combined*.

How can we say that? How can something as small as a smartphone be as powerful as radio, TV, and the personal computer combined?

Simply, because mobile provides *all three* of those things—and more—in a small device that can be put in your pocket. There's no need to be tied down to a big box that needs to be plugged in all the time. Instead, you and your customers can access it whenever you/they want and wherever you/they are.

Research by Morgan Stanley indicated that 91 percent of all mobile phone users have their phones within arm's reach 24/7.[1] Additional research by Nielsen shows that the growth of the iPhone was 10 times faster than the growth of America Online.[2]

The numbers get even more incredible. According to the 60 Second Marketer, there are 6.8 billion people on the planet, 4.0 billion of whom own a mobile phone. Do you know how many own a toothbrush?

3.5 billion.[3] That's right, *more people own a mobile phone than own a toothbrush*.

What's more, Gartner predicts that by 2013 the primary way people will access the Internet will be via their mobile browsers.[4] In other words, more than half the time someone accesses the Internet, he or she will be doing it from a mobile phone. That has huge implications for how your business needs to connect with prospects and customers.

Given all that, it's not surprising that you're curious about mobile marketing and that you're reading this book. After all, people like you have realized that mobile is going to be huge. No, wait. Strike that. Mobile *is* huge. And it's going to get even huger. (Is "huger" a word? Why, yes. Just Google it from your mobile device if you don't believe us.)

Is Mobile Marketing Right for You?

The starting point for anyone interested in diving into mobile marketing isn't to run out and develop an app or set up a mobile website. Instead, the starting point is to begin by asking yourself, "Is mobile marketing right for my business?"

With that in mind, we've come up with a handy little checklist designed to help you figure out if mobile is right for you.

Mobile marketing is right for your business if:

- ☐ You need new customers.
- ☐ You want existing customers to visit more frequently.
- ☐ You want to improve your profit margins.
- ☐ You need to appeal to a broader audience.
- ☐ You want to differentiate your brand.
- ☐ You'd like to improve your marketing return on investment (ROI).
- ☐ You want customers to spend more money each time they buy from you.
- ☐ You're looking for new distribution channels.
- ☐ You want to grow your market share.
- ☐ You want to be in front of your customers 24/7.

See where we're going with this? The odds are pretty good that one or more of the items listed here is important to you. Who doesn't want more customers? Who doesn't want to improve their marketing ROI? And who doesn't want to differentiate their brand?

FIVE MORE REASONS MOBILE MARKETING MIGHT BE RIGHT FOR YOUR BUSINESS

If the reasons just cited weren't enough to get you started in mobile marketing, here are five more that will almost certainly help you along your way:

1. *It's easier than you think.* Setting up, launching, and running a mobile marketing campaign is easier than you may think. If you're interested in getting a helping hand, reach out to a Short Message Service (SMS) service provider, your digital advertising agency, or a mobile ad network like AdMob, iAd, or Millennial Media. A quick phone call to any one of those entities will help you understand just how easy it is to get started in mobile marketing. Of course, reading this book will help, too.

2. *There's a huge untapped mobile audience.* The mobile audience is enormous, which leaves a wide gap between the number of marketers targeting mobile users and the actual number of people using mobile devices, like smartphones. This means that now is the ideal time to test out a mobile marketing campaign for your business, to see how effectively it can build your brand and sell your products.

3. *Mobile converts prospects to customers.* The conversion rate for many mobile marketing campaigns is dramatically higher than the conversion rate for traditional campaigns. eMarketer reports that 1 in 10 people currently redeem mobile coupons, which is 10 times higher than the redemption rate of some traditional coupons channels.[5]

4. *Mobile marketing costs less than traditional methods.* The cost of running a mobile marketing campaign is currently less than the cost of running many traditional marketing campaigns. Therefore, ROI of most mobile campaigns is higher than other marketing channels. What's wrong with a healthy ROI? Nothing.

5. *People respond to mobile.* Just as it's easy to start a campaign on your end, it's also easy for customers to opt in or respond to an ad through a click of a button on their smartphones. Easy sells; and more people are willing to reply to a text message or a mobile banner ad than are willing to clip a coupon out of a newspaper.

The bottom line is that there are amazing opportunities for any business interested in taking a dive into the mobile marketing pool. Better still, *mobile marketing is not that hard.* If you have a basic understanding of marketing, it'll be a piece of cake. And even if you don't, it's incredibly easy to learn.

How We've Organized This Book

We've organized this book so that it covers the key strategies used in mobile marketing today. That said, most of our focus is on tactics—in other words, *actionable* techniques that you can put to use tomorrow. You won't read much about "new paradigms" and "quantum leaps" as much as you'll learn how to "do this" and "do that."

We've organized the book in four distinct segments:

◆ Part I covers the mobile landscape and discusses some of the best practices used in various mobile marketing case studies.
◆ Part II outlines how to set up your business for success in mobile media.
◆ Part III goes deep into each of the tactics used in mobile marketing.
◆ Part IV discusses business-to-business (B2B) mobile marketing, mobile ROI, and the core characteristics of all successful mobile marketing campaigns.

There's a lot to digest in this book. Ready to get started? Great. So are we.

Notes

1. www.moyostudios.com/news/computers-and-consoles-to-become-obsolete; accessed October 25, 2011.

2. www.slideshare.net/BMGlobalNews/the-state-of-mobile-communications-5068995; accessed October 25, 2011.
3. www.60secondmarketer.com/blog/2011/10/18/more-mobile-phones-than-toothbrushes; accessed October 25, 2011.
4. www.gartner.com/it/page.jsp?id=1278413; accessed October 25, 2011.
5. www.mobilemarketingwatch.com/one-in-ten-users-redeem-mobile-coupons-18438; accessed October 25, 2011.

Part I

The Mobile Marketing Landscape

Chapter 1

How to Jump–Start Your Mobile Marketing Campaign

If you're reading this right now, you're probably interested in learning more about mobile marketing and how to use it to grow your business. That's terrific. But you might also be interested in learning how to jump-start your mobile campaign to get things going *quickly*.

That's exactly how we think, too. We're not the types to spend pages and pages introducing concepts *before* delivering the meaningful, actionable information. In our opinion, business is moving too quickly to spend time reading broad-stroke overviews before introducing you to the specific tools and techniques.

With that in mind, we've decided to kick things off with a first chapter that can get you into mobile marketing without delay. That way, you can fire up your campaign rapidly, then relax while you take a deeper dive into the finer points of mobile marketing outlined in the upcoming chapters.

Six Quick Lessons about Mobile Marketing
Ready to get started? Great. There are six ways you can learn about mobile marketing and begin using it to grow your sales and revenues quickly.

1. Become a mobile marketing power user.
2. Set up and launch your mobile website.
3. Analyze how the Fortune 500 use mobile marketing.
4. Register your business on location-based services.
5. Run a mobile paid search campaign.
6. Run a mobile display campaign.

1. BECOME A MOBILE MARKETING POWER USER

This may seem like a no-brainer, but you'd be surprised how many people *talk* about mobile marketing but don't actively *use* mobile marketing. Oh, sure, they may understand the *concept* of mobile marketing, but they haven't used it enough to become a *mobile marketing power user*.

To begin, we encourage you to go out and scan a Quick Response (QR) code today. And to use Google Voice Search from your smartphone. And to download foursquare, WHERE, or SCVNGR (pronounced Scavenger), and to use one of those apps to *check in* at your favorite retail store.

How about downloading the Delta Air Lines app and using it as your boarding pass the next time you're flying with that airline? Or think about using the Starbucks Mobile Card to pay for your next cup of coffee? Or even using the augmented reality apps from Yelp or Lodestone?

Have you clicked through on a mobile paid search ad? Used Skype on your smartphone to talk with a friend? Or scanned a bar code using Amazon's Price Check app?

To become a mobile marketing power user, you'll have to take a deep dive into it. In order to really *understand* mobile marketing, you're going to have to *use* mobile marketing. Otherwise, you won't really have a grasp of all the nuances of this amazing and powerful new tool.

2. SET UP AND LAUNCH YOUR MOBILE WEBSITE

If you haven't set up your mobile website already, we have some good news: It's easier than you might think. All it takes is a basic understanding of a few different approaches and then selecting the one that's best for you.

First, a little background: After several years during which the industry was trying to figure out whether .mobi sites were going to dominate, it looks as though m. subdomains or regular domains like .com, .org, and .edu, with subdirectories like .com/mobile, will be the primary format for mobile websites.

That's not to say that there won't be some .mobi sites; it's just to say that the landscape has sorted itself out and it looks like m. subdomains or regular domains will be the dominant format.

That leads to the question: How do you actually create a mobile website? What's the process for doing so? And how complex is it?

There are three simple solutions for setting up and launching your mobile website. The first is to use one of the automated systems offered by many web hosting companies. These systems essentially take your existing content and reformat it for a smaller screen.

Mobile Website Plug-ins for WordPress and Drupal

If you use a content management system like WordPress or Drupal for your blog or website, there are some mobile website plug-ins you can install that reformat your blog nicely so that it's mobile-friendly. These plug-ins do a surprisingly good job of taking your blog posts and packaging them in a mobile-friendly format.

As you might imagine, the end result is not perfect, because these tools take content that's written for a regular website and, essentially, repackage it to present on a mobile screen. Since visiting a website from a smartphone is an entirely different experience from doing so via a PC, this system is less than optimal.

For example, mobile visitors aren't usually interested in the kind of in-depth information they might search for on a desktop. Typically, they're in their cars, in the lobby of a building, or walking down the street. They're *mobile*. Thus, any mobile website that is simply a reconstituted version of your regular website is going to end up being a disappointment for you and, worse still, for your customers. That is why we suggest avoiding any automated system that simply regurgitates your existing website onto a smaller screen. There are better options out there.

One of those options is to use one of the plug-and-play systems provided by a variety of organizations. Some of the best companies for this include Mobify, Wirenode, Mippin Mobilizer, Onbile, and MoFuse. Alternatively, if you run your website using the HubSpot platform, your site is automatically mobile ready. Its system is set up so that your website is recreated for a mobile screen.

The companies just mentioned are very good, and are run by people who really know what they're doing. Some of them can help you with other aspects of mobile marketing, such as app development or mobile ad campaigns.

That said, there are some real clunkers out there, too. They're just one step removed from the automated systems mentioned previously. So be sure to investigate these kinds of companies thoroughly. You can start by visiting *their* mobile websites (from your smartphone, of course). Then take a look at some of their clients: Are they reputable businesses? Are they companies you admire? If so, visit those mobile sites and check them out, as well.

Of course, the best option is to have a web designer create a mobile site specifically for your company. If you have a regular website, you probably already have a web designer. And if you have a web designer, then he or she should be able to add a simple line of code to your home page that "sniffs" out whether your visitor is coming from a PC or smartphone.

Here's how that line of code works: When someone visits your website from a smartphone, the screen he or she is viewing it on typically is less than 600 pixels wide. If he or she is visiting it from a PC or tablet, the screen is typically more than 600 pixels wide.

Mobile Tip

Mobile marketing is constantly evolving. Here are three e-newsletters that provide very solid daily or weekly mobile marketing tips:

> ◆ Mobile Marketer Daily
> ◆ Mobile Commerce Daily
> ◆ Mobile Marketing Watch
>
> For sites that provide a broader range of marketing tips, you might find the HubSpot blog or 60 Second Marketer e-newsletter helpful, too.

By adding a line of code to your home page, your website can sniff out the width of the screen and determine whether the person is coming from a smartphone or PC. If the visitor is coming from a PC, he or she is directed to the regular site. But if the person is coming in from a smartphone, then he or she is directed to pages on the site that are specifically designed to fit on a smartphone.

The smartphone pages should be simple, clean, and easy to navigate. Keep in mind, as we mentioned earlier, a person visiting your site from a smartphone is expecting a very different experience from a person visiting your site from a PC.

3. ANALYZE HOW THE FORTUNE 500 ARE USING MOBILE MARKETING

Why should the big companies have all the fun? One of the advantages of mobile marketing is that it can be used by companies of all sizes. Take a look at what the Fortune 500 are doing and borrow liberally from their bag of tricks.

You'll find that most of them have mobile-optimized websites, and that many of them are using 2D codes, mobile paid search, and display (banner) ads. They're also probably using foursquare, WHERE, SCVNGR, or some other location-based marketing tool.

Take a look around at what they're doing and apply it to your own business. There's no law that says you can't repurpose their ideas to fit your own company.

4. REGISTER YOUR BUSINESS ON LOCATION–BASED SERVICES

If you haven't claimed (or registered) your business on services like foursquare, WHERE, and SCVNGR, you'll want to do so now.

Is It Worth the Trouble to Claim Your Business?

The short answer is, yes, you should claim your business. You never know when you'll want do to your own location-based promotion, even if yours is a B2B firm.

Besides, you don't want someone else claiming your business, do you? (Especially a disgruntled employee.)

Location-based services are mobile marketing platforms that businesses use to engage consumers and develop promotions. According to a study by Pyramid Research, location-based revenue in the United States is expected to climb from $2.8 billion in 2010 to $10.3 billion in 2015.[1] What does that mean to you? It means that if you haven't already jumped on board, you should do so now; your customers are using these services, and you should be, too.

All this begs the question, what does it actually mean to *claim your business* on a location-based service? Glad you asked. Claiming your business is just your way of raising your hand and saying, "I'm an official representative of this business and I want to claim its position on your service before any unofficial representative does."

Claiming your business is sort of like in the old days when you'd call up the Yellow Pages to confirm your listing. The only difference is that today you're confirming your listing online with a digital entity rather than with a traditional print publication.

When customers use foursquare, WHERE, or SCVNGR, they basically check in when they arrive at your business. Checking in is simply the process of opening the app from a smartphone and then clicking on an icon to let the business know the customer is at the location. Chili's leveraged this system brilliantly when it used foursquare to offer free cheese dip to everyone who checked in at its locations. Better still, the chain offered the same promotion to *everyone who checked in at any business within 200 yards of a Chili's.*

Yup, you read right. Chili's offered free cheese dip to people who checked in at any of the businesses that were within a 200-yard radius of any of its locations. The result was that it was able to draw customers in who might have otherwise eaten at a competitor's restaurant.

That's not only smart, it's downright brilliant.

5. RUN A MOBILE PAID SEARCH CAMPAIGN

According to a research study conducted by BIA/Kelsey Group, once searchers on a smartphone find a local business, 61 percent call the establishment and 59 percent visit the location.[2]

Those are some really monstrous numbers. Think about it: 59 percent of the people who find your business using mobile search ultimately will visit your location. Since that's the case, wouldn't it make complete sense to run a mobile paid search campaign for your business?

Paid search ads show up above the organic search results that are shown when you do a search on Google, Bing, or Yahoo! There are four best practices to keep in mind when you run a mobile paid search ad.

First, you need to "go local" and make sure your ads would appeal to searches from people who are either in their cars, on the sidewalk, or in a shopping mall. This is not to say that 100 percent of the people who do a search using their mobile devices are in their cars, on the sidewalk, or in a shopping mall, but the majority of them are, so it's a good idea to accommodate that.

The second is to be sure your ads click through to a mobile-optimized landing page. There's nothing more frustrating than clicking on a mobile paid search ad only to find the landing page isn't set up to be read on a smartphone.

The third best practice is to be sure your ads target immediate needs. According to MobileMarketer.com, 70 percent of mobile search users complete their tasks after one hour, compared to 30 percent on a PC.[3] That means target customers who are looking to fill immediate needs, at restaurants, bars, auto repair shops, big box retail locations, or bookstores.

Fourth, you'll want to broaden the scope of the keywords you select for your campaign. Since mobile search volume is significantly lower than that of online search, you'll need to include a broader range of keywords in your campaign in order to get the same kind of "umph" that you get with a traditional paid search campaign. You'll also want to include the word "locations" in your keyword list, as in "Pizza Hut locations" or "Walmart locations." And, finally, you'll want to include *urgency* terms such as "plumbing *emergency* repair" or "*24-hour* pharmacy."

In the end, you'll realize two things about mobile paid search: (1) It's not all that more complex than running a traditional search campaign; and (2) your competitors probably aren't using it yet, so you have an opportunity to acquire a lot of new customers they are missing.

6. RUN A MOBILE DISPLAY CAMPAIGN

Display ads are the small banner ads that show up when you surf the web on your smartphone. They're different from paid search ads, which are text ads that present when you do a Google, Bing, or Yahoo! search. Display ads look like tiny little banner ads and can include graphics, colors, and even motion.

What's great about mobile display (or banner) ads is that consumers respond to them better than traditional display ads. A recent research study found that mobile ads were opened by 61 percent of participants, whereas standard web ads were opened by only 7 percent of the consumers surveyed.[4]

This indicates that mobile ads have distinct advantages over traditional banner ads. First, they have the benefit of novelty, which is always a successful trigger for marketers. Second, they take up a larger portion of the browser page, so they have greater visibility.

The same study found that click-through rates spike between the hours of 7:00 and 11:00 PM each day. This seems to indicate a behavior we've all suspected for quite some time: *People don't use media in isolation; they usually use it in combination with some other form of media.* In other words, people don't just watch TV anymore; they watch TV and use the web at the same time. For proof of this, go find your teenager, the one watching *American Idol* while texting friends about the results.

You can get started using display ads by contacting one of the multitude of mobile advertising networks, some of which include iAd (from Apple), AdMob (from Google), Millennial Media, and Mobclix.

The Bottom Line: Get Started Today

In the end, the whole point of this jump-start chapter is to help you launch quickly into mobile marketing so that you can use it to attract new prospects and convert them to customers. After all, the main reason you're learning more about mobile marketing is so that you can use it to grow your business, right?

Growth is good. And mobile marketing can help you accomplish that.

Do This:

♦ Commit to *using* mobile media, in addition to simply reading about it.

♦ Sign up for an e-newsletter so you can stay up to date on this rapidly evolving marketing tool.

♦ Watch how other companies are using mobile marketing then *borrow* some of their ideas.

Don't Do This:

♦ Don't downplay the importance of mobile marketing (or any other new technology).

♦ At the same time, don't think that mobile marketing will solve *all* of your marketing problems. It's just one more tool in your marketing toolkit.

♦ Don't get started without defining your objectives first. What's your goal? Lead generation? Brand building? Customer conversion? Begin with the end in mind.

Notes

1. www.marketingpilgrim.com/2011/06/strong-growth-expected-in-location-based-services.html; accessed October 25, 2011.
2. www.mobilegroove.com/added-value-for-marketers-in-mobile-search-apple-itunes-purchase-data; accessed October 25, 2011.
3. Mobile Marketing Association, *Mobile Marketer's Classic Guide to Mobile Advertising, 3rd edition*, 2010, p. 61.
4. www.mobilemarketer.com/cms/news/research/10403.html; accessed October 25, 2011.

Chapter 2

How the Fortune 500 Use Mobile Marketing

Remember we recommended in the first chapter that you should study the way the Fortune 500 are using mobile marketing, and steal—sorry, borrow—some of their ideas? Well, there's no better time than the present to do that.

As you know, there are a variety of ways businesses can connect with consumers using mobile media. The most important are (Short Message Service (SMS) and Multimedia Message Service (MMS), mobile websites, mobile apps, mobile paid search, mobile display (banner) ads, location-based marketing, and 2D codes (QR codes, MS Tag codes, etc.).

Let's take a look at some of the ways companies around the globe have successfully used these tools to connect their brands with customers.

The American Red Cross Haiti SMS Campaign

One of the more famous—and more successful—mobile marketing campaigns was the Haiti Earthquake Relief effort run by the American Red Cross. More than 300,000 people died as a result of the 2010 earthquake, but many more would have perished if the American Red Cross had not used SMS to generate millions of dollars in donations.

When mobile phone users texted HAITI to 90999, they donated $10 to the American Red Cross. More than 3 million people gave to the campaign, 20,000 of whom opted in to receive ongoing e-mail communications. The organization was able to generate more than $32 million in donations during the life of the campaign.

Did You Know?

The Haiti campaign wasn't the first time the American Red Cross had conducted a Text2Give fund-raising effort. The first time was following Hurricane Katrina in 2005, but people weren't as familiar with SMS at that time, so that campaign didn't generate nearly the same results as did the one for Haiti.

What's even more impressive was that 95 percent of the participants were first-time donors. That means the American Red Cross engaged with 2,850,000 new "customers," who had never donated to the organization before. You can imagine the impact that had, and will have for many years to come.

The key takeaway from the American Red Cross campaign is that SMS can be used as a marketing tool *as well as an operational tool*. The organization benefitted on the *marketing* front with increased brand awareness and the acquisition of new donors. It also benefitted on the *operational* front because it opened up a new channel for prospects to donate to the organization, and made doing so much easier than it had been in the past.

HBO's *True Blood* Display Ad Campaign

Imagine you're a movie lover who is reading movie reviews on your Flixster or Variety mobile app. Suddenly, you notice that when you touch the screen, a bloody fingerprint appears. Then, when you touch the screen again, a second fingerprint shows up. Then a third one.

The next thing you know, blood is dripping down from the top of your screen. As it reaches the bottom, you see a pop-up ad, a call to action enticing you to watch a trailer for HBO's *True Blood* series.

It was a surprisingly innovative use of a new medium. How'd the campaign perform? Great! It helped increase viewership 38 percent, prompting more than 5.1 million viewers to watch *True Blood's* season-three premiere.[1]

The ad agency that developed the campaign took the iPhone applications from Flixster and Variety and adapted the apps to incorporate a message about the series. In addition, the agency worked with a mobile ad network called JumpTap to ensure the campaign ran across many other websites.

In the end, HBO embraced a new medium, created an innovative campaign that leveraged that new medium, and saw a 38 percent lift in viewership as a result.

The North Face Location–Based Marketing Campaign

Let's say you're an avid hiker, biker, or mountain climber who just happens to be toddling around New York City (as you're prone to do when you're not climbing Everest). The North Face recognizes that even when you're scaling the canyons of New York City, climbing Everest is always on your mind.

Definition: Mobile Ad Network

A mobile ad network is an organization that places your ads across a variety of mobile websites. The result is that you don't have to hunt down each individual website to run your ad; the mobile ad network does that for you.

So what did the outdoor clothing retailer do? It created a location-based marketing campaign using the Placecast Shop-Alerts system. Here's how it works: A customer (that'd be you) sees a poster inside a North Face store that says, "Opt in for text alert promotions when you're in our neighborhood. Opt out at any time."

Being the tech-savvy mountain climber that you are, you decide to whip out the old smartphone and opt in. Once you've done so, the

North Face uses *geo-fencing* to figure out your location. (Geo-fencing isn't that complicated. It uses three cell phone towers to figure out where you are by bouncing signals off your smartphone. The phone company is doing that all the time and now marketers are using the technology to make their messages even more relevant to the consumer.)

Now that the North Face (and your phone company) knows where you are, it can send you a text message about special offers the next time you're near one of its stores. The text message might read, "Welcome to San Francisco. Save 25 percent on sleeping bags during our 24-hour Labor Day promotion." Or it might read, "Welcome to Katmandu! Stop on by and get 20 percent off ice crampons for your next trip to Everest!"

Location-based advertising, Bluetooth Marketing, and location-based services are the next big waves in mobile marketing, so keep an eye out on these innovative new marketing tools. They worked for North Face and they'll probably work for you, too.

Intel's B2B Mobile Paid Search Campaign

Not all smartphone campaigns have to be about fancy websites or expensive app development. Sometimes, a strategy as simple as a mobile paid search can be extremely effective.

That's what Intel found when it ran a mobile paid search campaign using the Bing platform to support its "Meet the Processors" brand campaign. Covario, Intel's search agency, used *exact* and *broad-match* keyword search terms to drive people through to the brand's mobile website.

What were the results? Pretty impressive. The company found that Bing mobile search was 40 percent more cost-efficient than regular online search. Imagine what a hero you'd be if you walked into your CFO's office and said, "Hey, Big Shot. Guess what? I just saved you 40 cents on every dollar we're spending on paid search by using mobile search instead of regular search. So there!"

Of course, that statement would work even better if you didn't call the CFO "Big Shot," but you get our point: Mobile search is still an underutilized marketing tool, so dive in while it's relatively inexpensive.

Paramount's Shrek Display Ad Campaign

Over 50 million people visit Yahoo!'s mobile home page each month, which is about 1.5 million visits per day. (Yahoo!'s regular site generates about 140 million visits per month, or about 4.6 million a day.) Paramount decided to take advantage of Yahoo!'s high volume of traffic by creating a "rich-media" campaign around the release of the latest Shrek movie.

Visitors to Yahoo!'s mobile home page would see the top of Shrek's head along the bottom of their smartphone screens. When people touched the top of Shrek's head, the character would pop up and fill the screen. If they tapped Shrek's head again, they'd be redirected to the Shrek mobile microsite where they could buy tickets or see more information about showtimes.

Starbucks' E-Commerce Mobile Card

Okay, the Starbucks Mobile Card isn't really mobile marketing as much as it's mobile commerce, but the chain did such a good job making consumers comfortable with mobile payments that we just had to mention it here.

Here's how it works: Consumers download the Starbucks Mobile Card application to their phones. Then they load money into the Mobile Card, which keeps track of how much is on it. When consumers are in a Starbucks, they open the app and have the barista scan the bar code on their screens. If the coffee costs $4.99, then $4.99 is deducted from their Mobile Card balance.

There are a variety of cool things about this for Starbucks. First, having a mobile payment app for your store encourages customers to revisit the store so they can use it. Second, the mobile payment app increases brand loyalty because there's an emotional appeal to using an app from one of your favorite brands. And third, there's the marketing impact of engaging customers with the Starbucks brand in a new and innovative manner.

Adidas' Mobile Tracker Website

Approximately 30,000 people run the London marathon each year, and exactly 1,007,097 watch it from the sidelines. (How do we know it's exactly 1,007,097? We don't; we just get tired of writing "approximately" all the time.)

With that many runners and spectators, Adidas knew that there was an opportunity to engage a captive audience, many of whom would be interested in tracking the results of their favorite runners.

What did Adidas do? The sports apparel manufacturer created a Mobile Tracker website where users could enter a runner's race number and track his or her progress. The website was linked to the runner's RFID tags that were attached to his or her shoes. As the runner progressed along the marathon route, that data was recorded on a computer, which was tied to the website.

Spectators (all 1,007,097 of them) were able to track each runner's location, average speed, and projected finish time. In addition, they were given information on the course, how to navigate to different viewing areas, and the weather (which, in all likelihood, was drizzly and cool, since it was London).

The mobile website was used by nearly a half a million people to track more than 10 percent of all the runners in the race, giving Adidas a great deal of brand awareness and engagement during the process.

History Channel's Foursquare Campaign

Foursquare has more than 11 million members, and has generated more than 400 million check-ins, including one from space.[2] The History Channel recognized that foursquare check-ins provided the network a way to connect with potential viewers, so it created tips on foursquare that share historical facts with users when they check in at a particular location.

For example, when users check in to a location near Skylight Studios in New York City, they're informed that they're near the location where the world's first Otis Elevator was sold in 1853. By engaging people with facts about local landmarks, the History Channel was able to stay connected to both lovers of history and lovers of History (as in the network).

The New Jersey Nets' Gowalla Campaign

The New Jersey Nets wanted to create buzz and generate fan engagement using Gowalla, so it hid free pairs of virtual game tickets throughout New York City. The virtual tickets were located in sports bars, parks, and gyms, and could be exchanged for real tickets to a specific game. Attendees also won T-shirts and the chance for other prizes, too.

If your company is a hotel, airline, sports franchise, amusement park, water park, or any other venue that has leftover inventory during nonpeak periods, this kind of promotion is ideal. Think about it: The cost of giving away tickets to a nonsold-out basketball game is nominal, whereas the engagement and demand it generates among people who might not have gone to the game helps grow the customer base.

Hiscox's B2B Location-Based WiFi Campaign

Hiscox, an international specialty insurance company, launched a location-based WiFi campaign in the United Kingdom that integrated mobile display ads with an existing outdoor board campaign.

When businesspeople logged on to public WiFi in the vicinity of one of Hiscox's outdoor boards, they were greeted by a digital ad on their browser start-up screens that correlated with the existing outdoor boards in the immediate vicinity. In other words, if they logged on to the Internet while sitting at a restaurant in Covent Garden, the ads on the start-up screens matched the ads on the nearby outdoor boards. Both the Internet ads and the outdoor boards were specifically designed for people who were located near Covent Garden. The result was a double impact: first on the outdoor boards that were strategically located near the WiFi hot spots, and the second on the start-up screen that greeted people accessing the Internet using their smartphones, laptops, or tablet computers.

How did the campaign perform? Like gangbusters. The click-through rates on the location-based WiFi campaign were five times higher than the company's average rate for traditional online display ads.

Nissan's Microsoft Tag Campaign

Nissan wanted to figure out a way to promote its new electric car, the LEAF, in a way that would appeal to a target audience that was youthful, eco-conscious and health-oriented. So the auto manufacturer created an ad campaign promoting the "Innovation for Endurance" sweepstakes, featuring endurance runner Ryan Hall.

Definition: 2D Code

A 2D code is a mobile bar code that allows a smartphone camera to act as a scanner.

Specific kinds of 2D codes include QR codes, Microsoft Tags, SPARQCodes, and Data Matrix codes.

If you don't already have a 2D code reader installed on your phone, visit BeeTagg.com or SPARQ.it from your mobile web browser.

On the top left-hand side of the print ad, readers were greeted by a vibrantly colored Microsoft Tag 2D code. When the tag was scanned, it linked to a Facebook community showcasing Ryan Hall, as well as the latest innovations in running, cycling, yoga, and other fitness activities.

The purpose of the campaign was pure brand awareness and engagement. Nissan understands that getting potential customers to interact with its brand in some way, shape, or form is much better than simply allowing them to turn the page of a magazine. As a result, the company elected to drive people through to a Facebook page that continued the brand engagement, rather than to a mobile landing page where they could sign up for a test drive or be sold to in another manner.

All this brings up an important point about mobile marketing, and any other form of twenty-first-century marketing: It's important to first build a relationship with customers before you start selling to them. This is particularly critical if your target market is under the age of 35, since the youth market tends to resist the hard sell that was the hallmark of the previous century.

Fandango and MovieTickets.com Mobile Commerce Apps

What better use of mobile media than to give people the opportunity to purchase movie tickets on the go? That's what Fandango and MovieTickets.com realized early in the game.

The results have been amazing: 17.4 percent of the tickets sold for Paramount's *Transformers: Dark Side of the Moon* were purchased directly by using the apps, versus logging on to the MovieTickets.com website.[3] And 19 percent of the tickets sold for *Harry Potter and the Deathly Hallows, Part 2* were sold via the Fandango app.[4]

Why are these two case studies relevant to you? Because they show that mobile marketing isn't just about branding and advertising; it's about commerce, too. Simply put, the more transactions you can foster over a smartphone, the more likely it is that your campaign will pay for itself.

Domino's Pizza Delivery App

Domino's got burned early on in the social media by two rogue employees who uploaded a YouTube video that had a negative effect on its brand image. So if there was ever a company that you'd expect to be afraid of new technologies like social media and mobile media, it would be Domino's.

But to the pizza chain's credit (and that of its new CMO), Domino's has vigorously embraced social and mobile media: first, with an engaging TV and YouTube campaign that encouraged people to interact with the brand via multiple communications channels; and, second, with a surprisingly user-friendly mobile app that allows people to order pizza, customize their orders, and pay for them, all from their smartphones.

If you think about the actual complexity of ordering something as seemingly simple as a pizza, you'll understand how challenging it was to design an app that an ordinary consumer could download and use in a matter of minutes. Think about it: Domino's offers dozens of different toppings, cheeses, crusts, and sauces, which have hundreds of millions of potential combinations. (Seriously, do the math.) Yet the app makes the ordering process as simple and easy as possible.

Land Rover's Display Ad Campaign

Land Rover ran ordinary mobile banner ads that generated extraordinary results. The company's target audience is "high net worth males," so it ran ads on the AdMob mobile ad network (AdMob is owned by Google). The sites where the ads ran included CBS Sports/ News, AccuWeather, and other sites visited by the automaker's target market. In addition, AdMob targeted specific smartphones that were typically owned by high net worth individuals.

The campaign contained several possible actions for potential customers who clicked through on the "rich media" ads. For example, users could watch videos of the vehicles in action, view an image gallery, select their favorite-color Land Rover, and download it as wallpaper for their phones. Of course, they could also enter their zip code to look up the nearest dealer, enter their e-mail addresses to receive a brochure, or click-to-call for a scheduled appointment.

Definition: Rich Media

Rich media is digital advertising that moves, plays video, or is interactive in some way, shape, or form.

Traditional display (banner) ads are static and lack interactivity.

Rich media ads are more engaging and, as such, typically generate a higher click-through rate.

In the end, the campaign generated 45,000 video views, 7,400 customer wallpaper downloads, 128,000 gallery views, 5,000 dealer lookups, 800 brochure requests, and 1,100 click-to-calls.[5]

The Bottom Line

Now that you've had the opportunity to take a spin through some of the ways well-known brands are using mobile marketing to grow their sales and revenue, it's time to learn how *consumers* use mobile marketing.

The starting point for any successful marketing campaign is to think backwards and get inside the mind of your consumers. In the next chapter, then, we'll discuss how consumers use their smartphones in order to better equip you to create campaigns that match their usage patterns.

Do This:

♦ Study how corporations are using mobile media to connect with customers.

♦ Borrow the tactics that seem to work and ignore those that don't.

♦ Figure out how you can apply your knowledge to your own mobile marketing campaign.

Don't Do This:

♦ Don't assume that mobile marketing is just for large corporations with huge budgets.

♦ Don't default to boring, safe mobile marketing ideas. The more innovative is often the more successful.

♦ Don't assume that mobile marketing campaigns have to be expensive. Sometimes, as in the case of Intel and Land Rover, mobile marketing can be as simple as a paid search campaign or a mobile display campaign.

Notes

1. www.mobilemarketer.com/cms/news/advertising/6855.html; accessed October 25, 2011.
2. http://searchenginewatch.com/article/2081107/Foursquare-Hits-10-Million-Users-Yeah-Thats-1000-Annual-Growth; accessed October 25, 2011.
3. www.hollywoodreporter.com/news/movieticketscom-sees-surge-mobile-app-210358; accessed October 25, 2011.
4. www.mobilemarketingwatch.com/fandango-for-mobile-becomes-a-big-draw-for-the-box-office-this-summer-17287; accessed October 25, 2011.
5. www.admob.com/marketplace; accessed October 25, 2011.

Chapter 3

How Consumers Engage with Mobile

In the first two chapters, we walked you through how to jump-start your mobile marketing campaign and described some of the better mobile marketing case studies from around the globe. In this chapter, we're going to talk about how consumers engage with mobile media so that you can better connect with them as they use their smartphones.

Customers on the Move

Mobile customers don't have different desires and needs from the general population. In fact, given the current market penetration of mobile devices, they *are* the current population.

As more consumers use their mobile phones for more purposes, some mainstream forms of marketing may quickly become obsolete.

Considering starting a mobile marketing program? There are challenges to creating a community with "collective effervescence," the feeling that individuals get when they're part of a larger crowd with the same goals and desires.

Sporting events, political rallies, concerts, and rites of passage can all lead to opportunities to digitally evoke a feeling of joy and well-being, all centered on your brand.

With a world of information at their fingertips, consumers today are able to engage brands in a variety of new and creative ways, all on their own terms and at their own convenience. Realizing that consumer interest can be, at best, fleeting in the mobile world, the brands able to successfully capture and hold that attention through mobile-oriented consumer rewards, discounts, and promotional incentives are the ones that will win in the end.

Of course, to build and capitalize on the all-important mobile customer/brand relationship, marketers must figure out a way to meet both eager and not-so-eager customers at least halfway. With numerous mobile options currently available, figuring out how to engage consumers over the long term is what keeps marketers up at night. How can you provide content that is not only mobile-accessible but that can be phased into common usage? Let's talk about how consumers are currently using technology to engage their favorite brands.

Making the Connection

Before reviewing the type of mobile connections a consumer can make with a brand, it's important to note how these connections will be made. You may remember a time not too long ago when people owned mobile devices for making phone calls only. Today, mobile devices are used for shopping, watching videos, checking sports scores, playing games, and staying in touch with friends and families via social apps.

This means a user-friendly mobile website is the very first step for any brand or marketer wishing to develop an ongoing mobile relationship with its customers. In most cases, the brand simply needs to adapt its current web content for use with mobile browsers, and usually that means decluttering a page for simplified and smaller screens. Once this step has been taken, communicating the availability of your mobile-optimized website is important.

While a brand's standard website can be used to promote mobile readiness—and, in fact, standard websites can be coded in such a way to immediately forward mobile visitors from the standard site to the mobile version—this does little to inform potential users who have yet to make a connection. Luckily, mobile advertising and mobile search offer a means of reaching these consumers. Not only will a strong mobile search ranking make a brand more easily accessible to interested consumers, well-placed mobile ads also offer a targeted means of reaching potential customers.

Forming the Bond

No matter how consumers choose to engage a brand, be it via a smartphone, tablet, or other means, it is up to the marketer to provide an experience that encourages them to return time and time again. With mobile access, there is no shortage of ways in which consumers can spend their time; they're wired directly into an unlimited supply of information, including personal and work e-mails, local to world news, and social media networks. That's why relying only on brand loyalty, or the efforts to build brand loyalty, are tied to three specific elements: *strong content*, an *interactive experience*, and *user incentives*.

Depending on the brand, content may range from information regarding products and services to microblogging platforms, like Twitter. While relevant information can draw the user in, once that information has been obtained—or "consumed"—there must be a reason to return. Content can be shared and discussed openly, creating interactivity with the brand and establishing a community. When building the community, incentives can offer a means to ensure continued loyalty. Time-sensitive discounts, ongoing promotions, contests exclusive to mobile users, and mobile-only content are all ideal means of strengthening the relationship with the company or brand.

Means of Engagement

As means of engagement for smartphone users continue to multiply, brands might wish to consider how they can adapt. From simple opt-in SMS notifications to location-based QR or 2D codes, today's consumers are ready, and willing, to engage brands in a number of unprecedented ways. With that in mind, it's probably a good idea as a marketer to develop every possible mobile channel that could prove ultimately useful in connecting potential consumers with relevant content.

For example, location-based marketing can be a two-way street to consumer/brand engagement. Using QR/2D codes, brands can allow physically present consumers to scan products for additional online content using their mobile devices. From exclusive discounts to more detailed product specifications, the uses of mobile marketing technologies are limitless, making it an ideal strategy for brands seeking to facilitate engagement. In addition, using opt-in SMS or MMS strategies, brands have the capability to alert consumers to exclusive deals, product availability, content, and/or other incentive-based promotions on a local basis.

Meanwhile, smartphone apps allow consumers to engage brands in a variety of useful ways. From connecting via social media apps to browsing online stores, checking account information, and even making credit card transactions, never before have marketers enjoyed such a means of simply and effectively engaging with consumers.

Mobile Marketing Engagement

With many types of marketing, advertisers have approximately 30 seconds to make their presentations, which typically outline a problem/solution benefit of the product/service. With mobile marketing programs, advertisers may have as little as two seconds—the average time of a double-click to get their messages across. More than slightly overwhelming, don't you think?

Added to this shortened attention-grabbing time limit is that most mobile users will be engaged in another activity while they are using their phones. As they are sifting through the messages and information on their smartphones, they may be standing in line for a movie, waiting for a train or bus, going up or down in an elevator, walking along a sidewalk, or sitting at their desks. Talk about attention deficit disorder. This is a marketer's nightmare.

Because smartphones are used for conducting transactions, reading content, consuming entertainment, and acquiring information, today's businesses must learn to work within the limitations, and around the distractions, in order to make their mobile marketing effective. Limitations inherent when considering a mobile marketing program include:

◆ Very short time frame to gain attention to your message
◆ Mobile response action often combined with another activity
◆ Very, very small screen on which to present your message

Here are some tips for successfully using mobile marketing to engage consumers with your business or brand:

- *Set a goal.* Determine exactly what you want to accomplish with a mobile marketing program. Factor in that the user must absorb your content in the same amount of time it takes to double-click, or two seconds.
- *Pinpoint your target.* Research how users in your target market tend to use their mobile devices; for entertainment, or for reading their stock tickers?
- *Create a compelling call to action.* Your headline must be concise, strong, and short, conveying your point instantly while encouraging the viewer to learn more. Short copy rules in this medium.
- *Minimize page components.* Graphically overloaded pages will load slowly, so slowly that the user will move past your message to something else. Research shows that mobile users prefer to click rather than scroll.
- *Encourage sharing.* Getting a user to share your marketing message is quite possibly the most potent way of extending reach and increasing visibility.
- *Consider interactivity.* Adding interactivity to your mobile marketing message can help further engagement and convert visitors to customers. For example:
  - Click/text to call
  - Click/text to request sample
  - Click/text to request additional information
  - Click/text to enter contest or vote
  - Click/text to locate closest retail outlet
  - Click/text to receive discount or coupon
  - Click/text to download content

Engaging with Different Devices

Let's face it, you are going to use different devices for different applications. It only stands to reason that engagement with a home computer, a smartphone, or a tablet will require separate marketing applications for each use point.

Typically, when you sit in front of a computer, you are looking for more detailed information, easy navigation, and a larger, easier-to-read screen for your in-depth research. The websites you peruse at your desk will be larger and contain more pages. Chances are you will be somewhat blind to advertising on this device; and while you might be more interested in product reviews, specific product-related content, and other information related to your search, it's an entirely different experience from mobile use.

Turning to smartphones, you'll be more likely to use one to find quick information, local businesses, and check your e-mail or social media accounts. The smaller screen makes it more difficult to read detailed information, and mobile website load time is a crucial factor. While you may not be opposed to advertising on a smartphone, your expectations will be that the mobile site should provide basic information with easy navigation and click-through graphics.

Google reports that 81 percent of smartphone users access the Internet on their mobile devices (not a surprise, right?). And 50 percent use the Internet on their phones while waiting. More amusingly, 70 percent would rather give up beer than their smartphones if faced with that choice![1]

Tablet users take time for more leisurely activities, such as game playing, browsing, shopping, and content consumption. A recent Nielsen survey showed that tablets had the highest proportion of people using the device while watching television: 40 percent.[2] Tablet users are also more likely to watch video and read books; they also are more accepting of advertising and more likely to purchase after viewing an ad than are users on smartphones or other devices.

Most popular activities on tablets, according to AdMob, include gaming (84 percent), searching for info (78 percent), and e-mailing (74 percent). Least popular activities are shopping (42 percent), reading e-books (46 percent), and consuming entertainment (51 percent).[3] Even the least popular activities have amazing engagement levels across tablet platforms.

Within the mobile marketing field, there are unlimited options. All of these can be combined (with enough budget, people, and savvy), and work well together with the more traditional types of marketing programs. But, according to Google, 79 percent of large online advertisers do not have a mobile-optimized website.[4] This makes it difficult for mobile users to find what they're looking for, quickly and easily.

Mobile marketing considerations include:

◆ *Mobile websites:* A method for delivering content that focuses on the user seeking specific information
◆ *Mobile applications:* Typically, content or software that is downloaded—with permission, of course—by the consumer to their devices
◆ *Mobile messaging:* May be limited to text messages or may include images and audio for a richer experience
◆ *Mobile video:* Delivered via the mobile network; can be streaming or downloaded video

When you are thinking seriously about where to start with mobile marketing, remember that you have already begun; by reading this book you have set your mobile wheels in motion. But before you get any new project off the ground, think about education and preparation and remember that: 85 percent of mobile devices will be web-enabled by 2012, one in three mobile searches have local intent, and mobile search (according to Google) has increased 400 percent in 2011 versus 2010.[5]

You're very excited about mobile and what it can do for your marketing efforts, and it's up to you to spread the word. *Educate* your colleagues and managers about the powerful impact mobile can have on your online strategy. And don't stop there:

◆ Prepare yourself by defining your objectives. Ask what you want to achieve, both long and short term, with your marketing activities and within your business.
◆ Define the mobile marketing channel that will be best for your brand.
◆ Tap the right person or team to be responsible for running and reporting on mobile activity.
◆ Determine your budget and assess whether it is realistic.
◆ Most important, put metrics in place to ascertain the level of engagement or response rates, because "mileage will vary"

depending on the mobile channel and the actual marketing campaign itself.

Do This:

◆ Think small. Unlike many marketing programs, which are of the "go big or go home" variety, mobile efforts should be considered "bite-sized"—smaller screens, smaller messages can lead to big results.

◆ Think about what else the user is doing. Mobile users are almost always doing something else when looking at their smartphones or tablets. Recent ABI research stated that mobile users check their e-mail (80 percent), check weather or read news (63 percent each), play music or view stock quotes (53 percent each), check sports scores (51 percent), search for information (48 percent), or play games (39 percent).[6]

Don't Do This:

◆ Don't ignore mobile marketing. While not every business has the skill or money to develop a useful app, at the very least, one way to begin marketing your business is by creating a mobile-friendly website.

◆ Don't assume mobile marketing has nothing to do with your business. Mobile is here to stay. There are countless blogs, websites, and news media that stay current in this particular field of marketing. For a business to stay modern and competitive, marketing through mobile communication will be a critical part of its overall marketing plan.

Notes

1. www.telenav.com/about/pr-summer-travel/report-20110803.html; accessed October 23, 2011.
2. http://blog.nielsen.com/nielsenwire/online_mobile/40-of-tablet-and-smartphone-owners-use-them-while-watching-tv; accessed October 23, 2011.
3. www.guardian.co.uk/technology/appsblog/2011/apr/08/tablets-mainly-for-games-survey; accessed October 23, 2011.

4. www.google.com/think/insights/topics/think-mobile.html; accessed October 23, 2011.
5. http://searchengineland.com/microsoft-53-percent-of-mobile-searches-have-local-intent-55556; accessed October 23, 2011.
6. www.mobilemarketer.com/cms/news/research/10471.html; accessed October 23, 2011.

Chapter 4

Let's Talk

Terms and Concepts You Should Be Familiar With

O kay, so you're probably thinking, "A chapter on terminology? Really? Well, I can skip this bad boy and move on to the next chapter right away."

But wait.

Even though you may already know what SMS and MMS are, you'll probably want to familiarize yourself with a few other terms like *chat bot, acquisition rate*, and *predictive text*.

What's more, you'll want to understand some of the key concepts inherent to mobile and mobile marketing. After all, the primary reason you're reading this book is to learn *how to use mobile marketing to sell more stuff*, right? And if you're going to use mobile marketing for business, it's important to understand the key concepts of marketing in general.

Understanding Buying Behavior

Let's kick things off by talking about a primary concept: *how people buy products*. When you understand a little bit about consumer behavior, you'll be better able to convince people to buy your product instead of your competitor's product.

PEOPLE BUY PRODUCTS FOR EMOTIONAL REASONS, THEN RATIONALIZE THEIR PURCHASE WITH LOGIC

When a man walks into a Porsche dealership and drives away in a $150,000 car, do you think he buys the car because it has variable valve timing, or because he looks young and virile driving it?

When a woman buys a $10,000 Rolex, do you think it's because it tells time better than a $50 watch, or because it makes her look elegant and sophisticated?

People buy most products because of the way their purchases make them *feel*. In other words, they buy products for emotional reasons. But if you interviewed the man who bought the $150,000 car, and asked him why, he'd rationalize the purchase with *logic*.[1]

"I bought the Porsche because it has variable valve timing, 288 foot pounds of torque, and 345 horsepower."

Not.

The same holds true when people buy inexpensive products. A study at Baylor University asked 67 people to do a blind taste test of Coke versus Pepsi.[2] The results showed that about 50 percent liked Coke and about 50 percent liked Pepsi.

But when the university conducted a nonblind taste test—when people knew which brand they were drinking—75 percent of them preferred Coca-Cola. Why did this happen? It all goes back to what we said earlier: People buy products for emotional reasons, and Coca-Cola has more deeply ingrained emotional imagery than Pepsi does.

Here's a way to better understand the Coke versus Pepsi test results: Grab a sheet of paper and jot down all the words and phrases you associate with Coca-Cola. You'll probably come up with things like "happiness," "classic," "polar bears," "America," "Mean Joe Green," and "Santa Claus." (Santa Claus!)

When you do the same for Pepsi, the imagery is not as deeply ingrained. Celebrity names like Madonna, Michael Jackson, and Britney Spears probably come to mind.

So which is more deeply ingrained in the average consumer's psyche, Britney Spears or Santa Claus? Of course, the answer is Santa Claus, which Coca-Cola has been using since the 1930s to promote the brand.

The bottom line: People usually buy for emotional (branding) reasons, then rationalize their purchase with logic. (Side note: We're

Consumer Response Models				
Cognition Phase	*Attention*	*Awareness, Knowledge*	*Awareness*	*Presentation, Attention, Comprehension*
Affective Phase	*Interest, Desire*	*Liking, Preference, Conviction*	*Interest, Evaluation*	*Yielding, Retention*
Behavioral Phase	*Action*	*Purchase*	*Adoption*	*Behavior*

FIGURE 4.1   The AIDA Consumer Response Model, seen here in the second column from the left, is one of several response models that help explain the cognitive process people go through when they consider and purchase a product or service.

not saying people *always* buy for emotional reasons, nor are we saying they *only* buy for emotional reasons. We're simply saying that emotion plays a very significant role in the purchase process.)

UNDERSTANDING THE AIDA CONSUMER BEHAVIOR MODEL

Okay, now that we've explained the role emotion plays in the purchase process, let's talk about the cognitive process that happens when someone buys a product.

In the late 1800s, a gentleman by the name of E. St. Elmo Lewis developed a Consumer Response Model called AIDA, which stands for Attention, Interest, Desire, and Action. The AIDA model (see Figure 4.1) describes the process consumers go through when they engage with a product or service.

It wasn't long after Mr. Lewis brought the AIDA model to light that other people started to "improve" on his model. Many of these improvements have some validity, but for our purposes, let's stick with the AIDA model, since it does a good job of summing up what happens in consumers' minds as they go through the purchase process.

Converting a Prospect to a Customer

Another concept we'll discuss in this book is the idea of converting a prospect (or a lead) to a customer. When you create a mobile marketing campaign, you're often trying to persuade people to buy your product or service. (Sometimes, your intent is simply to create buzz or share information, but for our purposes, let's assume that you're trying to get them to buy something.)

When you run your campaign, you'll get some attention from people who are interested in your product or service. Those, of course, are your *prospects*. In many cases, those prospects will click a link, fill out a form, or visit your location. Once they've "raised their hand" and indicated that they're interested in your product or service, they're considered *leads*.

When leads actually buy your product or service, they've been *converted*, not in the religious sense, but in the sales sense. Once they're converted, they've become *customers*.

That whole concept of Prospect → Lead → Customer is an important one because it's the foundation for a lot of what we'll be talking about in the book.

Other Terms You Should Know

Now that we've covered some basic concepts, let's move on to vocabulary. These are the terms you should be familiar with if you want to become a mobile marketing superstar.

Ready? Here goes:

- *Acquisition rate:* The percentage of respondents who opted in or converted from prospects to customers. Acquisition rate = Total participants/Total audience. Also called the *conversion rate.*
- *Ad network:* An organization that places your ads across a variety of mobile websites. The result is that you don't have to go hunt down each individual website to run your ad; the mobile ad network does that for you.
- *Alerts:* Notifications containing time-sensitive information (e.g., event details, weather, news, services updates) that are pushed to someone who has opted in to receive the information.
- *Banner size:* The width and length of a display ad placed on the mobile web. It's typically presented in pixels: 305 px × 64

px and 215 px × 34 px are two common mobile banner ad sizes.

◆ *Blink message:* A message that contains blinking text for the purpose of emphasis.

◆ *Bluetooth:* A form of wireless communication that enables mobile devices to send and receive information over short ranges using the 2.4 GHz spectrum band.

◆ *Call to action (CTA):* Instructions to the recipient of a mobile marketing message to take action. "Call now" or "Sign up here" are typical CTAs.

◆ *Carrier (mobile carrier, mobile network operator, network operator, operator company, wireless carrier):* A company that sends you that whopping bill each month in return for access to its wireless telecommunications services.

◆ *Cascading Style Sheet (CSS):* An external document containing code that defines a website's appearance. (CSS is a term used most frequently by the guys in the web department.)

◆ *Chat bot:* A computer-generated response sent to chat participants. It sounds like a human, but it's not. Generally reserved for nonmobile websites, a chat bot is sometimes used on mobile sites as well.

◆ *Click-through rate (CTR):* A way of measuring the success of a mobile marketing campaign. CTR is obtained by dividing the number of users who clicked on your ad by the number of times your ad was delivered.

◆ *Click-to-call:* A link that enables a mobile subscriber to initiate a call to your business. Click-to-call links are a great way to increase in the number of responses to your ad or to the landing page on your mobile site.

◆ *Conversion rate:* The percentage of respondents who opted in or converted from prospects to customers. Conversion rate = Total participants/Total audience. Also called the *acquisition rate.*

◆ *Cost per thousand (CPM):* A metric used to price the cost of advertising banners. Essentially, a CPM is the price you pay for every 1,000 ad impressions delivered. CPMs typically range from about $6 to about $15 on up.

- *Double opt-in:* When someone initially opts in to your alerts or special offers, you send the person a confirmation, or double opt-in. It's sort of a polite way of saying, "Are you sure?"

- *Global positioning system (GPS):* This comprises the satellites and receivers that allow your cell phone to be located anywhere in the globe. Cell tower triangulation is another way to track a cell phone's location, but that's a different technology from GPS.

- *Impressions:* The number of times mobile subscribers have viewed a particular ad, text message, landing page, or website.

- *Landing page:* When someone clicks a link on a mobile ad, he or she is delivered to a web page called a landing page (sometimes called a *jump page*).

- *Location-based services (LBS):* These are services provided to you based on your location. They can include marketing messages, driving directions, parent/child monitoring services, and information about local restaurants, ATMs, movie theaters, and so on.

- *MMS message:* A message sent via a Multimedia Messaging Service that contains multimedia objects.

- *Mobile Marketing Association (MMA):* The global nonprofit trade association established to lead the growth of mobile marketing and its associated technologies. The MMA has more than 700 member companies from over 40 countries around the globe.

- *Mobile paid search:* A search campaign using Google, Bing, Yahoo!, or other search engine that is specifically run on mobile devices.

- *Near field communications (NFC):* A wireless technology similar to Bluetooth that enables the communication between devices over a distance of less than 10 centimeters.

- *Opt in/out:* When subscribers have given/refused their consent to receive some form of communication from you, they've opted in/out.

- *Paid placement:* Paying a fee to a web property to have your listing prominently displayed, typically as a sponsored listing.

- *Predictive text:* Intelligent software that predicts the text you're typing and makes suggestions based on those predictions. Also called *autocorrect*.

- *Preroll:* The streaming of a mobile advertising clip prior to a mobile TV/video clip. The mobile ad is usually 10 to 15 seconds in length.
- *Pull messaging (wireless pull advertising, content pull messaging):* Any content sent to you upon your request. For example, when you request the local weather from a website or app, the content of that response (including any ads) is pull messaging.
- *Push messaging (wireless push advertising, content push messaging):* Any content sent by advertisers and marketers to your mobile device at a time other than when you requested it. Push messaging includes audio, Short Message Service (SMS) messages, e-mail, multimedia messaging, cell broadcast, picture messages, surveys, or any other pushed advertising or content.
- *Short Message Service (SMS):* A fancy name for texting. Your teenager uses his or her mobile phone for SMS more than to call people.
- *Smartphone:* A mobile phone that includes features more commonly associated with computers or PDAs. They can store information, send and receive e-mails, include apps, and do a whole slew of other nifty things.
- *Vanity short code:* Short numeric numbers (typically 4 to 6 digits) that are specifically requested by a content provider. The code usually spells out a name, brand, or an associated word, or is an easy-to-recall number sequence (e.g., DISNEY = 347639).

Now that you understand the key concepts and terminology around mobile marketing, are you ready to move on?

Great. Let's go.

Do This:

- Ask yourself what people are really buying when they purchase your product or service. People don't buy Porsches only for the German engineering; they buy them because the cars make them feel young and virile. What are the emotional reasons people are buying your product or service?

- ◆ Get inside the mind of your consumer. What obstacles to a sale can you eliminate to help improve the AIDA process?
- ◆ Become comfortable with the terminology and concepts in this chapter. They'll come up again and again throughout the rest of the book.

Don't Do This:
- ◆ Don't take the concept of emotional purchases too far. There is logic involved in the purchase process; it's just that the primary driver is frequently emotion.
- ◆ Don't skip over this chapter. It's important to understand these terms and concepts, because we'll be using them throughout the book.

Notes

1. www.pickthebrain.com/blog/are-you-rationalizing-your-decisions; accessed October 24, 2011.
2. www.60secondmarketer.com/60SecondArticles/Branding/cokevs.pepsi-tast.html; accessed October 24, 2011.

Chapter 5

Nine Ways Businesses Are Using Mobile Marketing

Many people once considered mobile phones a novelty, but today they're considered must-haves. In many cases, mobile phones have replaced the more traditional computer landscape of laptops and personal and desktop models. Moreover, with mobile devices occupying the majority of user free time, ripple effects are being felt far and wide, especially when it comes to business and marketing. Where potential customers once stood idle, reading advertisements on the backs of shopping carts and browsing merchandise while standing in the register lines, today's consumer will most likely spend those few free moments connecting to the online world. With mobile devices ranging from smartphones to tablets, businesses large and small are just now beginning to realize that mobility is no longer a novelty, a future consideration. Mobile marketing is now, today, the present.

With the potential benefits of mobile ranging from customer acquisition to streamlined sales conversion, it's no wonder that mobile media has become a serious marketing tool for businesses of all sizes. Let's take a peek at nine ways that companies ranging from international airlines to family-owned car dealerships are using the far-reaching potential of mobile media in their marketing programs.

Short Message Service (SMS)

The most far-reaching and ubiquitous of data applications, SMS has so far proved to be the most successful mobile media tool for businesses. Cost-effective and easy to integrate, SMS capabilities provide a number of benefits to a variety of specific applications. Some of those benefits include:

- *Ubiquity:* With text capabilities at the fingertips of users worldwide, SMS offers the simplest and most cost-effective means of communication, be it with customers or internally within your company.
- *Compatibility:* Accessible to virtually all mobile networks and devices, SMS communications offer a worldwide audience, creating maximum flexibility no matter your product, service, industry, market, or geography.
- *Personable:* Offering a form of communication that is both personal and interactive, SMS can involve customers in the process, generating a sense of brand loyalty while also establishing your brand as a reputable channel of mobile interaction.
- *Environmentally friendly:* By phasing out paper communications, SMS alleviates the strain on the environment of printing and mailing direct response vehicles.
- *Cost-effective:* SMS is a very inexpensive messaging alternative to other types of marketing campaigns.

SMS communications are useful in a wide range of internal and external applications, including:

- *Community dialogue:* Create a sense of community through live conversations with customers or colleagues.
- *Content:* Entertain or inform your audience with easy access (via a link) to content including e-books, videos, music, and games. Depending on your purpose, SMS can be used to inform your database of content updates or new product information.
- *Promotional campaigns:* Hold text-to-win contests or voter-based competitions, or engage customers with personalized discounts and virtual rewards.

- *Time-sensitive information:* Keep valuable contacts abreast of stock quotes, scheduling, travel arrangements, and account transactions.
- *Authenticate identification:* Secure access to sensitive customer information by validating the identity of the requestor.

Multimedia Messaging Service (MMS)

A new standard in mobile messaging, MMS is another way to send a message from one mobile phone to another. The main difference (of course, there *had* to be a difference!) between MMS and SMS is that MMS can include not just text, but also sound, images, and video. It is also possible (and here's where it gets really interesting from a marketer perspective) to send MMS messages from a mobile phone to an e-mail address.

Nearly all new smartphones manufactured with a color screen are capable of sending and receiving standard MMS messages. Brands can deliver (mobile-terminated) and receive (mobile-originated) rich content in the continuing effort to encourage engagement, participation, and ultimately, results.

An interesting example of mobile-originated content is Motorola's ongoing mobile campaigns at House of Blues venues. The program combined on-air and on-site into a truly unique online execution, resulting in a 99 percent participation rate! Consumers sent their mobile photos to the installed LED display, and text messages were posted in real time during the concert—all to win cool sweepstakes prizes such as seating upgrades and artist meet-and-greets.

Near Field Communications (NFC) and Bluetooth

NFC and Bluetooth allow for simplified transactions, data exchange, and connections with a touch. Many smartphones currently on the market already contain embedded NFC chips and Bluetooth technology that can send encrypted data a short distance ("near field") to a reader located, for instance, next to a retail cash register.

Interest in NFC has surged, primarily because Google recently joined a cadre of wireless carriers, banks, and credit card companies planning a number of ways to use the technology for mobile payments in the United States. Today, many consumers may be scanning QR codes to connect via mobile to promotions and mobile web pages, but as a greater number of consumers adopt NFC, you'll see consumers simply wave their phones over NFC chips embedded in posters, point-of-purchase materials and check-out payment processors.

Free Tool: Check Whether Your Website Is Mobile Optimized

HubSpot offers a free tool to determine (among other cool marketing information) whether your standard website is optimized for mobile viewing.

Visit WebsiteGrader.com and enter your Website URL into the simple, single-form field at the top of the page.

The multipart Website Grader report will help to identify areas for improvement and indicate where you rock!

Mobile Websites

An established web presence isn't enough to make mobile an automatic part of your marketing program. You need to provide your mobile web users with an experience that is both prompt and user-friendly. Unfortunately, the average, standard website does not translate well to the smaller screens of mobile devices. "On the go" Internet access provides several advantages, such as the ability to communicate via e-mail with others and obtain information anywhere. Some nonmobile-optimized websites require excessive scrolling; have increased load-time lag on mobile devices; limit message size; and are unable to access pages that require a secure connection, host Flash, or have PDFs (although Flash and PDF access have been improving of late).

Today's customer would rather access product and service information online than call directly or visit a store in person. Believe it or not, the inherent drawbacks of viewing a standard (nonmobile-optimized) website on a mobile device is simply too frustrating for mobile users to bear.

When you stop to consider the growth of smartphones and how they are expected to outpace ownership of other computing devices within a couple of years, why would you risk losing business because of a negative mobile web experience?

Primary considerations for a mobile website include:

* *Use smaller pages* to keep information on screen and easily accessible for the mobile user to scan.
* *Create simpler layouts* to decrease web page load times and minimize user frustration.
* *Establish mobile browser compatibility* across multiple platforms.
* *Provide information* in a manner that is quick, clear, and concise.
* *Encode your standard site* to automatically recognize and transfer mobile users to your mobile site.

Mobile Display Advertising and Paid Search

With potential customers constantly in motion, mobile display advertising and paid search methodologies are playing an increasingly important role in the world of mobile devices. By placing advertisements on relevant mobile websites and paying to be included in mobile search engines, businesses are much more likely to catch prospects during some part of their buying cycle, increasing the likelihood of conversion to customers.

While these marketing methods are similar to the ones used in the standard world of pay-per-click (PPC), creating a separate mobile campaign allows the marketer to devise a more finely targeted and media-appropriate approach. By segmenting ads based on demographics, location, or even the user's choice of mobile device, a clear sense of the market can be created, allowing the advertiser to home in at an unprecedented level of accuracy.

Advertisers are now able to clearly measure the success of a mobile campaign. The relevance to the customer—Does the content and messaging reflect the user's lifestyle, interests, and buying habits?—is determined in real time as a personal interaction. To be most effective, it's important to keep the characteristics of mobile users in mind. For example, mobile searchers are less likely to type in longer search terms, so an emphasis on shorter queries that can be easily searched via mobile devices would be useful. And when trying to increase your marketing budget ROI with mobile, consider vying for a top position when advertising, as the small viewing area of a mobile website allows for only a limited number of ad displays.

Search is going mobile. The number of people accessing the web on their mobile phones is skyrocketing. Searching on a mobile device is different from searching on a desktop or laptop computer. The screen is smaller and typing can be a hassle.

Within the broad umbrella of mobile search, there are a range of services, including:

- *Mobile-optimized search engines*: Google, Yahoo!, and Bing have launched "mobile-friendly" versions of their search engines.
- *Mobile Q&A services:* A type of organic search engine, these include Question Mania (questions answered via text by a real person) and the U.K.'s MyHelpa, which reverse-bills SMS messages to connect to a human search agent.
- *Mobile directory search:* Also known as "Find my nearest" or "Mobile Yellow Pages," the services use location-based technology to pinpoint where the mobile user currently is (or should be).
- *Mobile discovery services:* Similar to recommendation engines such as Amazon.com, these services offer mobile users thoughts on what they should do next, as in recommending a similar restaurant to one just searched for.
- *Mobile navigation services:* Primarily defined by mobile operators, these services provide content to users outside their operating portals.
- *Dynamic Mobile Selection Interface Services:* A newer category of mobile search is one in which a preselected set of possible search content is downloaded in advance by a mobile user, and then allows for a final search step. Think push button, without the need for text entry, search, result review, or page scrolling.

Location-Based Marketing

Location-based marketing programs are a terrific way to draw in a variety of potential customers, whether they're local or happen to be visiting from out of town. Not only is this method particularly advantageous for customer acquisition, it can work to your advantage in building customer loyalty and repeat business. The key to getting started in this area is to provide location-based social networking sites with relevant and accurate information, to help potential customers find your place of business.

Once you've been able to draw likely customers to your doorstep, there are many ways to enhance the customer experience, increase your potential for generating revenue, and encourage repeat business, including:

◆ Promotional discounts and giveaways for initial check-in and repeat visits
◆ Ongoing promotions where incremental discounts and special prizes are awarded based on the number of customer check-ins
◆ Targeted promotions through social network sites such as Twitter or Facebook

Making use of real-time promotional campaigns while customers are physically in the store can help your business with customer feedback and generate word-of-mouth advertising (how radical is that concept—talking to another person?) as they share their experiences via social media. In addition to enhancing the customer shopping experience (and who doesn't want that?), location-based marketing also provides the marketer with an opportunity to target engaged consumers in the moment, when they are much more likely to make a purchase.

In addition to converting sales and building positive customer relations, location-based marketing can help your company stand out as a cutting-edge brand that rewards tech-savvy customers, effectively differentiating your products and services from the competition. What's more, both the costs and risks associated with this aspect of mobile marketing are so negligible that it makes sense, especially when stacked next to earlier variations of this same concept: the many plastic loyalty cards hanging off our key chains and filling our wallets.

Mobile Apps

Mobile applications have a tremendous upside when it comes to marketing potential, a fact that businesses have quickly recognized. With the population of smartphone users ever growing, and the capabilities of mobile devices daily increasing, apps offer unlimited possibilities in terms of expanding business opportunities and improving personal productivity.

Try This: QR Code/2D Code

Did you know 14 million people scanned a QR code in June 2011, up 400 percent versus the year prior?

FIGURE 5.1

Visit SPARQ.it, download its QR code reader, and scan the QR code shown in Figure 5.1 to learn more interesting facts about QR or 2D codes.

The key to a successful application is customer value. If your app is not compelling and useful to your customers or prospects, it will be quickly forgotten, or even ignored, among the much more interesting competition. That is why it pays to design an app that offers vital information, but in a way that is not overwhelming to the first-time user. As your customers adapt, you can tweak the app accordingly to offer more value, service, or support. Of course, it's important to remember the adage "Jack of all trades, master of none"; in the world of the app user, an application that performs one task well is of much greater value than the app that inadequately attempts to perform several.

Today's smartphone users have access to a wide variety of task-oriented applications that have ultimately affected the daily operation of businesses worldwide. Effective use of these apps can improve customer relations and your bottom line (not too shabby, huh?). Consider the inherent benefits of some time- and money-saving business-oriented smartphone applications:

◆ Keep track of tax-deductible business expenditures.
◆ Synch up with personal and business computers for instant access to all customer- and account-relevant information.
◆ Create invoices or accept credit card payments on the fly.
◆ Keep track of accounts and cash balances, and take advantage of text alerts for payment due dates or irregular account activity.

QR Codes/2D Codes

Two-dimensional (2D) codes offer business owners the opportunity to provide huge amounts of information in the smallest of spaces. Similar to the one-dimensional bar code, which holds up to 20 numeric digits of information, 2D codes can communicate thousands of characters to smartphone users by implementing the scanning capabilities of their built-in camera functionality. There are a variety of different kinds of 2D codes, some of which include QR codes, SPARQ codes, and Microsoft Tags. Not only can these codes provide information, they can link consumers directly to web-based content via the smartphone's mobile browser.

The applications of QR/2D codes are numerous and amazing. Consider these possibilities:

◆ Direct potential customers to your online or physical store.
◆ Bring offline customers online.

- Create a sense of community with customers via links to social media and mobile web content.
- Use QR/2D codes as a promotional vehicle, with special discounts for users.
- Provide product information, recommendations, and up-to-date contact information to improve customer service.

To ensure the success of your QR/2D code campaign, be sure to carefully consider the placement of your codes. Popular locations include:

- Business cards
- Promotional literature, such as data sheets
- Product tags
- Trade show signage
- Product packaging
- Print advertising
- Ticket stubs
- Receipts
- Storefront signs and windows
- Company vehicles (cars, trucks, trailers)

Remember, it's not necessary to overwhelm customers with information. QR/2D codes should be used to provide quick access to information that customers and prospects will find useful, relevant, and rewarding. What's more, landing pages or offer pages on your website can be updated to provide the latest information on products, services, and promotions. If done right, QR/2D codes can encourage repeat business and show a significant ROI.

Tablet Computing

Convenience is quickly making tablet computers the go-to mobile device of the executive world. Allowing hands-on interaction with relevant business information, this cutting-edge technology offers all of the advantages of laptops without the added weight and hassle of transport. What's more, they're longer-lasting and more powerful than smartphones, which also come with the inconvenience of a tiny screen and keyboard.

Tablet computer owners claim numerous advantages of their devices, including:

♦ Maintain direct connection to e-mail and other web-based content, including social media.

♦ Keep contact information and calendar up to date and store other sensitive information.

♦ Enjoy remote access to personal and business computers for easy access to important business-related e-mails, documents, and programs that may not be accessible via other alternatives.

♦ Create documents and presentations on the go, or add last-minute changes to ensure your info is accurate and up to date.

♦ Easily view documents, presentations, and web content on tablet screens, or hook directly to HDTV through the HDMI port.

♦ Connect to a printer when documents must be shared physically (how 2009!).

♦ With the appropriate application, turn your computer tablet into a scanner using an on-board camera, or set up a video conference.

♦ Keep track of finances such as stocks and banking and credit accounts.

With a larger screen, tablets offer many of the advantages of smartphones; plus, you can see everything! No matter the size of your business or the size of your screen, mobile media offers a wealth of opportunities that simply cannot be overlooked.

Do This:

♦ Think about which of the nine ways businesses are using mobile media today make sense for you and your marketing efforts, then pick one to start with. Choose one that won't cause too much damage to your budget or your health.

♦ Make sure you communicate your objectives and the success/failure of your program to your entire team. For mobile to work well within the marketing mix, clarity is important. Often, marketers forget the internal audience when they launch something new and awesome.

◆ Gather your forces. Encourage employees of your company, members of your family, and fans of your products/services to participate in this new program.

Don't Do This:

◆ Don't try to do everything. Especially all at once. If mobile is not part of your marketing mix now, take baby steps. You'll be happier knowing that you tried and succeeded, step by step.

◆ Don't insist on doing the most difficult task first (such as creating a new app). Find out what your customers are doing with mobile, figure out something cool to help them, and then deliver on that promise.

Note

1. http://blog.trakqr.com; accessed October 23, 2011.

Chapter 6

Classic Mobile Marketing Mistakes You Can Avoid

The traditional definition of mobile marketing is any marketing technique that moves or is mobile, such as moving billboards, typically appearing on trucks.

Today's definition of mobile marketing revolves around marketing techniques on or with mobile devices such as cell phones or smartphones. In 25 years, U.S. wireless market penetration of mobile devices climbed from less than 1 percent in 1985 to 38 percent in 2000 to 96 percent today.[1] Recognition of the extraordinary influence of mobile as a marketing platform, and its associated "real estate," is now a reality. Another reality—an unfortunate one—is the common misuse of the very small available space and the inherent ineffectiveness of using that space as if it were the average highway billboard!

Your mobile marketing campaigns will be more meaningful with a mobile website that enjoys compatibility, optimized content, usability, and good design. To achieve that level of quality, there are several classic marketing mistakes you should avoid while planning your mobile marketing strategy. We've outlined the key ones in this chapter, and recommend that you keep them in mind as you plan your mobile campaigns.

Treating the PC and Mobile User the Same

Just as there are oblique differences between offline and online, there are differences between mobile and traditional Internet marketing, and failing to recognize them could produce less-than-optimal results. Mobile marketing programs or campaigns require a change in approach, based on the platform and the user.

Mobile marketing is:

◆ *Fast:* Users need to consume your information quickly and while on the move. Therefore, information should be kept brief. It may be logical to present a five-page PDF document for the desktop version of your website, but not so sensible for a download from your mobile version.

◆ *Succinct:* Present your information in a manner that is easy to recognize and comprehend. Wordiness, lengthy explanations of your product or service, will not be valued on the small screen.

◆ *Creative:* The prime, yet very limited, availability of space requires that you use graphics and images that can be easily interpreted for marketing messaging. Judicious use of icons is part of that creativity.

◆ *Location:* Consumers who visit your mobile website from their smartphones are on the go. Many of them will be looking for directions (or a map) to your location, or your phone number. Make sure you acknowledge your consumers' needs by including click-to-map and click-to-call icons on your mobile site.

Failing to Recognize Differences in Mobile Equipment

Just as thousands of words and massive file downloads are a turnoff for the mobile user, failing to understand and respect the limits of the mobile device is another potentially fatal mistake when designing a mobile marketing campaign.

Several issues to consider when planning your strategy:

◆ *Bandwidth limits:* Keeping file size small is important when planning a mobile marketing program. Many providers restrict data usage and/or have very slow download speeds.

- *Charges and fees:* There are providers using flat data usage rates; however, many still charge per byte used. You'll find that users will not want to waste their money on insignificant information.
- *Keyboard and mouse:* While there may be a stylus (less and less likely), there won't be a mouse for your smartphone. And a full-sized keyboard doesn't exist. This means limiting the screen movements to up-and-down scrolling, and minimizing the need for extensive typing (long forms do not work in this environment).
- *Printers:* When possible, allow users to complete a task without having to move away from the mobile platform. Users are more likely to fill out a short form on their smartphones and hit the enter or submit button than take the link, copy it, e-mail or text it back to their desktop computer, download and then print out the form, fill it in, scan it—you get the idea. Whew!

Other Common Mobile Media Mistakes

The limits to designing for the mobile device are balanced with unique ways to integrate its capabilities into the mobile marketing platform. A smartphone is a phone (obviously); a camera and a video camera; a GPS device; a music player, a calendar, a video player, a game console, an e-book reader—you get the picture (no pun intended).

Integrating these disparate capabilities with linkages to your mobile website can create a rich and interactive user experience. This integration is what forms the basis for a holistic marketing campaign, making mobile more powerful as a tactic and a strategy component. By integrating online and offline methods, mobile and traditional websites, mobile pages, 2D codes, and SMS messaging, you will build a marketing campaign that not only will encourage your loyal customers or users to follow your brand across multiple platforms but will act as a magnet for prospects (not yet customers)!

Here are a number of additional mistakes marketers are making with their mobile efforts, with a consideration toward correcting them:

- *Looking for magic:* There isn't a mobile marketing campaign in the universe that will produce instant gratification overnight. It takes time, patience, and continued effort to build a strong following and show revenue. Yes, it would be nice to have a silver bullet, but that is not likely for any long-term success, is it? Instead of throwing your mobile program against the wall to see if it sticks, try continuing with separate offers and calls to action, different types of campaigns, or unique channels, in an effort to show progress. Stick with it and the magic will come.

◆ *Seeking perfection:* Let's face it, nothing is perfect. We try and try for that one flawless campaign—polishing, tweaking, emphasizing—only to come away disappointed when the long-hoped-for results are not there. What to do? Remember, marketing, really successful marketing, is a continual process with short- and long-term goals. Every ad, every offer, every campaign may have some degree of measurable impact, but you need to consider the "air cover" your efforts are providing. Go out on a limb and the results will provide a benchmark for future efforts.

◆ *Putting all your marketing eggs in one basket:* We have to assume that you are reading this book because you want to create mobile marketing programs. But mobile should not be the sole component of your organization's marketing efforts. Consider reserving mobile as part of a greater strategy that includes tactics such as websites, e-mail, and print. Think about integrating Quick Response (QR) codes in a print ad or pushing the reader to your website to get an instant coupon or take a virtual tour of your company.

◆ *Mobile-spamming your audience:* It is relatively easy, and certainly cost-effective, to send frequent mobile messages to your prospects and customers. But at what cost? Consider that the average recipient is well versed in e-mail spam; receiving multiple SMS or text-based messages from your company will not endear it to the prospect. Think instead about creating a well-thought-out campaign that sends messages occasionally. Sending the message less frequently will make the recipient more likely to take notice—and take action.

◆ *Failing to make the medium "exclusive":* Most people end up joining a mailing list (direct mail, e-mail, social, mobile, etc.) simply because they are looking for information. It could be the customer is looking for a deal or another value-add promotional consideration. Or it could be the consumer is looking for the right timing to make a purchase decision, and nurturing this opportunity will turn the prospect into a customer. It is tempting to promote the same offers that may be getting airplay from your other marketing campaigns, but try to avoid this trap. By offering exclusive "mobile-only" discounts, content, rebates, and so on, you may be able to phase out older, higher-cost marketing programs and generate more revenue.

◆ *Being concerned about the size of your mobile list:* What constitutes a "big" list? A thousand? Ten thousand? A million? Seriously, a large number of names on your list does not automatically equate to a corresponding level of sales. Conversely, a small number of opt-ins to your mobile database does not mean zero revenue. Here's an example from HubSpot:

> *While working to promote the World's Biggest Online Marketing Seminar, in conjunction with the launch of Dan Zarrella's new book,* The Contagiousness of Ideas, *HubSpot's marketing team offered a special opt-in to a VIP SMS program. In response, 359 people texted "opt in" to a special code; two days later, when a free Kindle download of Zarrella's book was made available, 14 percent clicked through. Compare that mobile click-through rate with standard e-mail CTRs of 2 to 3 percent.[2]*

Instead of worrying about how many names you have on a list, consider working on the engagement level or interaction with the ones you do have. By continually growing your list with exclusive offers, you will add to it at the same time you increase your reach.

◆ *Treating mobile as a one-way street:* It's relatively simple to send out mobile messages that do not require replies; and usually this marketing mode makes sense, especially for exclusive coupons or special announcements. However, if you are looking for more interaction, you could use your mobile list to ask questions, request feedback via a simple poll, or survey the timing of your messages.

◆ *Living the hype:* How many companies do you know that invest resources in creating an app and then promote it everywhere, only to discover the hype doesn't match the value? You see this fairly frequently these days in marketing efforts geared to build a Facebook page for a business; but, ultimately, the page serves little purpose. Remember that it might be better to start small, with a simple program, and determine the level of interest on the part of your audience before jumping into a developer maelstrom with an application.

◆ *Forgetting how your audience uses mobile search:* Searching for products and services on your desktop is an entirely different experience from searching online with your phone. A mobile search that results in information downloads and PDF documents will not be a satisfying experience for the person searching for your company. Typically, mobile searchers want quick access to relevant information and, often, location-aware experiences for specific activities. Keep your mobile site streamlined, with just the essentials on the home page.

◆ *Forgetting it's mobile, not e-mail:* Similar to the previous mobile marketing mistake, many marketers are in a PC frame of mind when designing mobile marketing programs. When you send an e-mail newsletter to your prospects and customers, you load it with valuable content to encourage incremental products and services knowledge and to nurture the recipient on an ongoing basis. The same cannot be expected from a mobile user; thus special consideration has to be part of your planning. Think succinct.

◆ *Ignoring mobile's limitations:* Small screen, no mouse, no printer, limited keyboard, and restricted bandwidth: Keep these restrictions in mind when designing campaigns for a mobile device and the result will be a more mobile-friendly website.

Additional tips for mobile websites include:

◆ Use portrait instead of landscape format in the design.
◆ Use a single, left-justified text column instead of horizontal tabs and text columns.
◆ Use a second-level domain name such as GoMobileBook .mobi.

- Use Extensible Hypertext Markup Language (X-HTML) when programming your website, to ensure that any web browser will be able to render your site optimally.

Do This:

- Test your regular website for mobile readiness before launching a mobile marketing campaign. Use WebsiteGrader .com as a means to determine whether you're ready or not.
- Make your mobile website searchable and findable. A mobile-ready site will allow search engines to index your content in a format that makes it easy to read on a mobile device.
- Promote your mobile website so that prospects and customers can find valuable offers easily.

Don't Do This:

- Don't promote your website as mobile-ready if it is not.
- Don't treat your mobile opt-ins the same as your e-mail subscribers.
- Don't give up. Start small; set realistic goals.

Notes

1. http://gs.statcounter.com/#mobile_os-ww-monthly-201007–201107; http://blog.nielsen.com/nielsenwire/online_mobile/in-u-s-smartphone-market-android-is-top-operating-system-apple-is-top-manufacturer; accessed October 23, 2011.
2. www.lyris.com/e-mail-marketing/85-Average-E-mail-Click-Through-Rate; accessed October 23, 2011.

Part II

Setting Yourself Up for Success

Chapter 7

Laying the Foundation for Successful Mobile Marketing Campaign

When builders construct a house, what's the first thing they do? Do they frame the house? Install the doors? Build the chimney?

Nope. The first thing they do is to *lay the foundation*. If you put down a good, solid foundation, then you know that the frame and the doors and the chimney will all stay in place.

So before we dive into some of the specifics of developing a mobile marketing campaign, let's lay the foundation for success by taking a look at a number of marketing fundamentals that'll help you along the way.

The Marketing Mix

In 1953, Neil Borden coined the term "marketing mix."[1] It's a concept that includes several aspects of marketing, all geared toward building awareness and generating customer loyalty. The Four Ps are part of the marketing mix.

The Four Ps and the Five Cs

You may already be familiar with the concept of the Four Ps, which are *product*, *price*, *place*, and *promotion*. Nevertheless, let's take a quick spin through them here before we move on to an equally important concept called the Five Cs.

◆ *Product*, the first P, is what you're actually selling to the consumer. This can be something tangible, like a book, toothpaste, or a T-shirt; or it could be something intangible, like accounting services, web design services, or even a vacation on a cruise line.

◆ *Price*, of course, is the amount a customer pays for your product or service.

◆ *Place* is the location where the product or service can be purchased. It can include brick-and-mortar locations as well as e-commerce sites on the Internet.

◆ *Promotion* represents all of the communications you might use to let people know about your product or service. There are four distinct elements to promotion:
  • Advertising
  • Public relations
  • Personal selling
  • Sales promotion

The Four Ps became an important part of the marketing vocabulary around the 1960s and helped marketers stay focused on the four most important components of their marketing programs. You'll want to keep the Four Ps in mind as you develop your campaigns, whether you're using traditional marketing tools (like radio, TV, or print) or some of the newer tools (like social media, paid search, or mobile marketing).

Now let's talk about another important concept: the Five Cs. These can help you analyze both the internal and external factors influencing your marketing program. Use the Five Cs as a way to identify where your strengths and weaknesses are.

Let's take a quick look at all five:

◆ *Company* includes your product line, your image in the marketplace, your experience, your culture, and your goals.

Essentially, it's the "stuff" you're stuck with for the short term since items in this category usually take a long time to change or alter.

- *Collaborators* are the companies you're doing business with. These include distributors and suppliers, and even alliances you have with other corporations.
- *Customers* are, of course, the people who buy your products and/ or services. You can analyze your customers based on market size, growth potential, tangible and intangible benefits, motivations behind the purchase, and value drivers; whether they're decision makers or influencers; where they get their information about your brand; what their buying process is and their frequency of purchase; and other factors that influence their buying behavior.
- *Competitors* include your direct and indirect competitors. Your *direct* competitors are the companies that offer a product or service that is very similar to yours. Your *indirect* competitors are companies that offer a product or service that competes for your customer's share of wallet. (For example, Pepsi is a direct competitor to Coca-Cola; and both companies would consider Popsicle as an indirect competitor because consumers who are looking for refreshment might easily choose a Popsicle over a soft drink.)
- *Climate* comprises all of the macroenvironmental factors that influence your success or failure. These include the political and regulatory environment, the economic environment, the social environment, and the technological environment.

We've covered a lot of ground over the past few pages in addressing the Four Ps and the Five Cs, so let's do a quick recap. The Four Ps were invented in the 1960s as a way to look at the key elements of a marketing campaign. The Five Cs were formulated later as a way to deepen your understanding of your overall marketing program. Both are important, but if you're going to focus on one or the other, direct your efforts at the Five Cs.

Why People Buy

We talked earlier about the fact that people buy most products or services for emotional reasons and then rationalize their purchases with logic. Now let's take a deeper plunge into consumer behavior and explore the differences between what people *say* and what people *do* when they choose one brand over another.

If you conducted a survey and asked participants what they looked for in a bank, one of the top answers would be *financial security*. If you asked them what they looked for in a restaurant, a good percentage of them would say *cleanliness*.

That's all fine and dandy, but if you developed a marketing campaign for a bank or a restaurant based on these answers, you'd be horribly disappointed with the results.

Why? Because people *expect* banks to be financially sound and they *expect restaurants to be clea*n. That's the *price of entry* to participate in the marketplace. If you ran an ad for a bank that said, "We're *not* financially sound, but we do offer free checking," it would be out of business in no time. Again, people *expect* banks to be financially sound and they *expect* restaurants to be clean.

A better approach is to analyze your product or service *differentiators*, those factors that make your product or service stand out from your competition.

Alan Deeter, strategy director of the go-to-market strategy company Dangerous Kitchen, helped develop a list of 20 questions to identify *brand differentiators*. It's a great list you can use to figure out what will help your product or service stand apart from that of your competitors.

Here's the list of questions. The best way to benefit from this list is to gather a group of your key executives in a room and hash out the answers. (You'll be surprised at how few of your executives will agree on the answers.)

1. What are we at present?
2. What do we want to become in two to five years?
3. What is our greatest opportunity in the next two years?
4. Why is that such a great opportunity?
5. What would we need beyond our company's current strengths/positioning/products to seize the opportunity described above?
6. What is our greatest threat?

7. Is this a threat we can control? If so, what should we do to control it?
8. What do we do better than anybody else?
9. When we win, why do we win?
10. How does our customer benefit from what we sell?
11. What are the top three reasons customers have bought our products or services?
12. What are the typical objections to a sale? In other words, when we don't gain a new customer, what is the reason given?
13. What percentage of next year's revenue is expected from new versus existing customers?
14. Going forward, what are the essential attributes of our target customer? (Industry segment, size of organization/corporation, demographics, job position, motivators, internal and external influencers, buying habits, key message points, factors in buying decisions, associations, publications, trade shows.)
15. Who are our key competitors?
16. What type of work do we most enjoy?
17. Who is our competition targeting?
18. How do we wish to be viewed in relation to our competition?
19. What is the typical sales cycle?
20. What values, personality, and attitude do we want to project?

Putting Your Differentiators to Work

Figuring out what your brand differentiators are is an important exercise, one that can have a significant impact on your brand.

In the 1990s, the Coca-Cola Company came up with 35 different attributes or differentiators for its flagship product. These differentiators included attributes like *refreshing, sociable, trendy, modern, funny, simple, reliable, consistent, emotional,* and *everywhere.*

Each of these attributes appealed to a different segment of Coke's target audience. As a result, the company came up with ads for each of them and ran them simultaneously. The result was a 55 percent increase in sales after just five years.[2]

Admittedly, not everyone is in a position to afford 35 different ads for each of their products' attributes, but the point is still valid: When you identify what it is that makes people choose your brand over another brand, you can increase sales consistently, whether you're in the business-to-consumer (B2C) world or the business-to-business (B2B) world.

So far, we've covered the Four Ps, the Five Cs, and the importance of differentiating your brand. Now let's talk about another important topic in the world of consumer behavior, called *stated versus derived importance.*

Stated Importance versus Derived Importance

As mentioned previously, just because someone states that financial stability is important for a bank doesn't mean that it's an effective driver for customer acquisition or brand loyalty.

A better way to find out what will drive sales is to ascertain what actually *causes someone to buy your product or service.* In marketing research circles, this is called *derived importance*, which establishes how specific attributes correlate with customer behavior.

If someone says "low price" is an important reason to shop at a particular clothing store, and shops there regularly, then that would be an indicator that what he or she says (stated importance) and what he or she does (derived importance) have a high correlation. That's good.

When you compare what people say (stated importance) with what they do (derived importance), you can learn a lot about what actually drives sales for your product or service.

There are four different combinations of stated and derived importance, which can be plotted out on a map that looks like the one shown in Figure 7.1.

Key drivers are attributes that are high in both stated and derived importance. If you have good performance in both areas, you'll have strong sales. For example, people often say that "good value for the money" and "excellent-quality food" are important for a restaurant (stated importance), and their behavior would indicate that this is true (derived importance). As such, "good value for the money" and

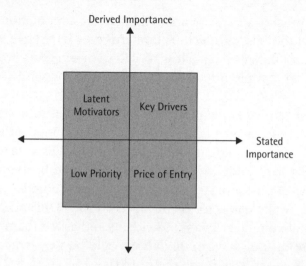

FIGURE 7.1 By examining the stated versus derived importance quadrants, you'll be able to find out what actually drives sales for your product or service.

"excellent-quality food" would be considered key drivers for a restaurant.

Price of entry attributes are those high in stated importance but low in derived importance. In the restaurant example, people will almost always say that clean restrooms are important, but using that as a key differentiator for your restaurant won't help much. In other words, people *expect the restrooms to be clean*, so that's considered a price of entry into the category.

Latent motivators are the hidden reasons people buy your product or service. This is where you can mine for gold.

Let's take an example. It would be uncommon for a male or a female survey respondent to admit that he or she frequents a restaurant because he or she finds the servers attractive, but— trust us on this one—that's a key differentiator for many, many restaurants. Attractive servers are a latent motivator; people may not mention it as a top attribute in survey responses (stated importance) but it definitely shows up as a reason people frequent a restaurant (derived importance).

These latent motivators work in the B2B world, too. There's an old saying that "nobody ever got fired for hiring IBM"; in the days when IBM had total dominance in the mainframe computer world, it was the "safe" choice. The company had the best reputation, the best service, and the best product. The alternatives may have been less expensive, but they were also less well known—in other words, they were a risk. So people hired IBM because they knew it was the safe choice.

That's not the only example of a latent motivator. If you have a B2B sales force (or even a B2C sales force), a latent motivator for your company's success is going to be a highly intangible factor called *likability*. It's hard to define what makes someone likable, but it's a combination of trust, honesty, charm, and a low-key sales approach. Likability is what sells a lot of products in the B2B and B2C sales worlds. But if you interviewed individuals and asked them why they bought a product or service, *likability* would be way, way down on their list of reasons they made the purchase.

Thus, *likability* is a latent motivator; it's a factor with low stated importance, but high derived importance. It's important, even though people don't fess up to its importance in surveys.

Low-priority attributes are low in both stated and derived importance. For example, if you sell running shoes and you offer free shoelaces with every purchase, that's not going to make much difference in whether or not someone shops at your store. In other words, it won't show up in either the stated or derived importance category.

Building on Your Marketing Foundation

The concepts discussed in this chapter are important because they lay the foundation for the development of your mobile marketing campaign. In upcoming chapters, we'll talk about how to think strategically about your campaigns. Simply put, there's no sense in developing a mobile marketing campaign if you haven't thought through your objectives and your strategies for reaching those objectives.

Do This:
- Gather a group of your key executives in a room and use Alan Deeter's list of 20 questions to help you establish your key differentiators.

◆ Conduct research to find out which of your brand attributes show up in the stated importance category or the derived importance category.

◆ If you're not in a position to hire a research company to do a stated versus derived importance analysis, then you'll want to do the analysis based on your own experiences.

Don't Do This:

◆ Don't assume you have deep insights into your customers. Talk to them directly (formally or informally). Also, ask your sales force for their insights into your customer's behaviors.

Notes

1. http://en.wikipedia.org/wiki/Marketing_mix; accessed October 24, 2011.
2. www.consumerpsychologist.com/marketing_introduction.html; accessed October 24, 2011.

Chapter 8

Getting More Familiar with the Mobile Marketing Landscape

If you're planning to go mobile, you'll need an in-depth understanding of the various tools and platforms at your disposal. With that in mind, we thought this chapter would be a good place to take another lap around the mobile marketing pool so you can deepen your understanding of what's out there.

Understanding Smartphone Operating Systems

Every mobile device needs an operating system for it to work. There are a number of operating systems used around the globe, including Apple's iOS, Google's Android, RIM's BlackBerry, Nokia's Symbian, and Microsoft's Windows Phone.

We've broken out the market share for the top four operating systems in several countries around the globe in Table 8.1. This delineation should give you a sense of which operating systems are the most popular in your part of the world.

Let's take a look at three of the more popular operating systems in the United States and see what differentiates each from the others.

TABLE 8.1 Top Four Operating Systems[1]

Country	Most Popular	Second Most Popular	Third Most Popular	Fourth Most Popular
United States	Android (39%)	iOS (28%)	BlackBerry (20%)	Windows (9%)
United Kingdom	BlackBerry (41%)	iOS (37%)	Android (16%)	Symbian (4%)
Australia	iOS (72%)	Android (18%)	Symbian (7%)	Windows (1%)
Brazil	Symbian (42%)	Unknown (21%)	Samsung (20%)	Android (8%)
Canada	Apple (46%)	Symbian (22%)	BlackBerry (19%)	Android (8%)
China	Symbian (42%)	Unknown (37%)	iOS (12%)	Android (5%)
Egypt	Symbian (76%)	iOS (6%)	Unknown (5%)	Android (4%)
France	iOS (58%)	Android (28%)	Symbian (5%)	Bada (2%)
Germany	iOS (54%)	Android (29%)	Symbian (7%)	Sony Ericsson (3%)
India	Symbian (69%)	Samsung (15%)	Unknown (9%)	Sony Ericsson (3%)
Japan	iOS (48%)	Android (42%)	WAP (6%)	Unknown (3%)
Russia	Symbian (45%)	Android (16%)	iOS (14%)	Unknown (10%)

[1]http://gs.statcounter.com/#mobile_os-ww-monthly-201007–201107; http://blog.nielsen.com/nielsen wire/online_mobile/in-u-s-smartphone-market-android-is-top-operating-system-apple-is-top-manu facturer; accessed October 24, 2011.

Google's Android

It's hard to argue with an operating system created by the geniuses at Google. Android is an app-centric operating system, meaning that, like Apple's iOS (described next), it features apps front and center. There are also several hard buttons across the bottom of each Android device, to bring up the Home screen and others.

There are more than 100,000 apps for Android, which can be found in a variety of places including the Android Market. There are third-party app markets, too, as well as the ability to download and install apps straight from the web without having to go through any marketplace.

Android doesn't have restrictive policies about development tools used to create its apps. For the most part, this open policy is a positive, because it enables more rapid innovation on the part of developers. But it can also be a negative; since no single entity vets the apps prior to publication, some of them can be a bit sketchy.

At one point, several dozen Android apps were even pulled off the market because hackers had written and developed apps with malware in them.

Another downside to Android's open operating system is that manufacturers and wireless providers can customize it in any way they want. This means they can clutter the phones with trinkets and trash of no interest to you. But overall, the open approach that Google uses with Android has more benefits than detriments, which is part of the reason that Android is the most popular operating system in many parts of the world.

Apple's iOS

There's only one place to install apps for the iOS and that's at an Apple Store. Apple has chosen to be much more cautious in its approach to its apps and operating system. Getting apps approved through the rigorous Apple process is labor-intensive, but the end result is often worth it.

The Apple iOS does what Apple does best: It creates a simple, intuitive, and elegant experience that makes using an iPhone a snap. But that simplicity has some drawbacks. Although users of the Android system can customize their phones to a greater degree than users of the iOS, Apple insists on a clean, uncluttered approach to its user experience, so this ability to change features based on a user's likes and wants is sometimes limited. That said, the iOS Settings app gives users control over the fundamental features of the phone, including brightness, WiFi use, sounds, and other features.

Another drawback is that the guidelines restricting certain apps from making it through Apple's rigorous approval process can sometimes be applied inconsistently. For example, Apple allegedly banned some apps that featured women wearing bikinis, but then turned around and reportedly gave *Sports Illustrated* the green light to use similar images. Other developers have complained that they are not given easy-to-follow recommendations on how to fix their apps that get rejected.

But in the end, the Apple iOS is what it is: an amazing operating system that changed the rules on what it means to be a smartphone.

Windows Phone

Instead of the app-centric approach you'll find in the Android and iOS operating systems, Windows has organized its OS around *information* rather than *apps*. Users will find large buttons, or tiles, designed to give them access to information, rather than access to an application. In some cases, the tiles might deliver updates from your friends on Facebook, or the next appointment on your calendar. In other cases, they link you to the information you're looking for about your contacts or the weather.

There aren't as many apps available on the Windows Phone operating system, but with tens of thousands of available apps, who has time to try them all out anyway? Also, Microsoft has followed Apple's example regarding the openness of its operating system. For now, the only place you can download and install apps is from Microsoft's store, but that may change in the future.

One of the strengths of Windows Phone is that it integrates seamlessly with its applications and cloud-based services. There's a version of Outlook built into the operating system, and it works quite smoothly. And Mobile Office does a terrific job of integrating Word, Excel, PowerPoint, and other Office apps right into the phone.

Getting to Know the Carriers and Manufacturers

The role of the carriers and manufacturers in a mobile marketing campaign isn't a huge one, so we won't spend too much time on it. That said, it never hurts to be familiar with the players in the industry.

AT&T, Verizon, and Sprint are the three largest carriers in the United States. When you include T-Mobile's subscribers in the AT&T mix, they claim about 43 percent market share. Verizon has about 34 percent, and Sprint has about 21 percent.[1]

The manufacturers include companies like HTC, Motorola, Samsung, HP, Apple, RIM BlackBerry, and Nokia. RIM and Apple manufacture 100 percent of the phones that use their operating systems. Google and Microsoft, on the other hand, purchase their phones from HTC, Motorola, Samsung, and HP.

In the long run, it helps to be aware of the carriers and manufacturers, but as a marketer or a business owner, there are plenty of other things to keep your eye on first before exploring much deeper into the carrier and manufacturer world.

Apps and App Development

There are a number of good reasons companies spend money on app development. They may want to raise brand awareness among customers and prospects. They may want to increase customer retention and loyalty. The may want to expand sales channels and make mobile shopping easier. Or they may simply want to attract and keep customers longer in a physical location.

Now that you have a sense of why businesses invest in apps, it's a good time to get to know the world of apps a little better.

In this section you'll find a list of dozens of the top applications that can be downloaded onto your smartphone. (For the complete list, visit the 60 Second Marketer website from your smartphone and click on the "100 Top Mobile Apps" icon.)

We've broken down the list into these categories: News and Information, Social Applications, Games, Culture/Fun, Shopping, Branded Apps, Productivity Apps, Financial Tools, Organizers, and Utilities.

Take a spin through these to get familiar with them. Better still, download them onto your smartphone and use them!

Here goes:

News and Information
- *ABC News Mobile:* This application is for all those who love to be in the know. You can receive text alerts about breaking news, watch video, listen to podcasts, or read articles, all on your mobile phone.
- *AccuWeather:* Downloading the AccuWeather app allows you to view a two-day forecast based on your GPS coordinates.
- *Caffeine Finder:* The name says it all. Perfect for people who need their daily (or hourly) fix.
- *ESPN Mobile:* Recently named Mobile Marketer's mobile publisher of the year, ESPN's offering of mobile media applications has something for every sports fan, including games, articles, and live TV.

- *Fast Food Finder:* Wouldn't it be great if there were an app called "Healthy Food Finder"? Until then, there's Fast Food Finder.

- *Google Books:* Interested in rereading the Declaration of Independence or Dante's *Inferno?* Download Google Books to your smartphone and you're ready to roll.

- *Google Maps:* What would men do without Google Maps? They'd have to ask for directions—which, of course, will never happen. Fortunately, Google invented its Map app for guys (like me) who are too stubborn to stop and ask directions.

- *The Huffington Post:* The mobile version of this popular online news and opinion publication features breaking news, blogs, and original content.

- *Kindle:* You can use your smartphone to preview books that you might like to buy later. Clean and customizable, the app permits you to preview the first chapter, as well as add bookmarks, notes, and highlights.

- *Pandora:* Are you a music lover? Then you're probably already familiar with Pandora. Pandora allows you to create your own radio station based on your specific tastes. Check out the Liberace Channel! (Kidding).

- *Qik:* A new, faster way to share videos with all of your friends, Qik allows you to record and instantly upload videos to the Internet, or stream live video straight from your phone. You can also two-way video chat or send video mail.

- *Stitcher:* This mobile application lets you get your news on the go by streaming up-to-date audio content about business, sports, politics, and entertainment.

- *The Weather Channel:* The Weather Channel's app and the mobile version of weather.com provide up-to-date weather information, text alerts, animated maps, and more.

Social Applications

- *Bump:* This is a terrific application that allows you to exchange contact information, photos, social networking information, and calendar events just by "bumping," or touching, your phone with another Bump user.

◆ *Facebook:* You can update your Facebook page on the fly with its mobile version. You can even update your Facebook Places profile, which lets people know where you're eating, drinking, relaxing, or just hanging out.

◆ *Foursquare:* Ready to "check in" to your favorite restaurant, bar, mall, or retail store? It's a great way to get discount coupons from the stores you frequent the most.

◆ *Gowalla:* Much like Yelp, Gowalla allows you to browse through the best restaurants, bars and other entertainment sites in your neighborhood.

◆ *HootSuite:* Using HootSuite, you can manage your Facebook and Twitter accounts within an elegant, clean user interface. HootSuite stands out from other social network managers for its extra features: You can schedule updates, set columns to monitor keywords and hash tags, and translate updates into other languages.

◆ *LinkedIn:* Interested in staying connected with your business contacts? If so, then the mobile version of LinkedIn is for you. It's perfect for trade shows and events and for people on the go.

◆ *Loopt:* Allows you to connect with your friends by sharing your location and status with friends. With Loopt, you can find your friends on a map and view their photo and status updates in real time.

◆ *Skype:* Verizon Wireless users can now use Skype through their phones with free Skype-to-Skype calling and IM without using their mobile minutes. Users with other carriers can get a Skype To Go number that they can reach from any mobile phone.

◆ *Twitter:* You don't have to be sitting behind a desk to update your Twitter status. The mobile version lets you stay connected wherever you are.

◆ *WordPress, TypePad, or Drupal Blogging Platforms:* Interested in writing a blog from your hammock, your sailboat, or your private island? You can do it with these mobile apps. (But first you have to buy a hammock, a sailboat, or a private island.)

◆ *Yelp:* This application can give you restaurant reviews on the fly. Better still, its augmented reality mobile application lets you look through your mobile screen and places tags with reviews over the restaurants on that street. In other words, it overlays information about each restaurant over a live view of it, seen through your viewfinder.

Games

- *Angry Birds:* This addictive game, where you get revenge on the green pigs who stole the bird's eggs, has reached the number one spot for paid apps in over 60 countries.
- *Tap Tap Revenge:* Similar to Guitar Hero, this game tests your rhythm as you tap out beats and shake left and right as the arrows fall.
- *Words with Friends:* This crossword game allows you to match wits with your friends or one of the millions of people in the Words with Friends community.

Culture/Fun

- *Fandango:* This movie-lover essential allows you to search movie showtimes, buy tickets, and watch trailers.
- *Happy Hours:* Displays the best food and drink deals going on near you at any time each day. You can filter results in a number of ways, including by day, time, location, type of cuisine, and special features like free WiFi and outdoor seating.
- *RunKeeper:* You can track your workouts in a fun, easy-to-understand way with RunKeeper and then share them with friends.
- *Shazam:* Do you often find yourself wondering what song is playing on your radio? Shazam not only identifies the song, it also allows you to purchase it straight from your phone.
- *YouTube:* You can now check out the latest YouTube craze straight from your mobile phone. You can search for and watch videos, or record and upload your own videos.

Shopping

- *Amazon:* If you're at a trade show or in a meeting and someone mentions a hot new business book, wouldn't it be great to be able to order it right then and there? With Amazon's free mobile phone app, you can order it on the fly.

- *eBay:* No need to lose a bidding war because you're on the go. With eBay mobile you can search, buy, pay, and check the status of your eBay activity on your phone.
- *Scoutmob:* This website allows you to have coupons for local stores and restaurants sent to your phone, which you can redeem simply by showing the cashier the text message.
- *ShopSavvy:* You can use your phone's camera to scan any bar code and receive a list of prices and inventory information for the same product at local stores and online retailers, ensuring you get the lowest price every time.

Branded Apps

- *Bank of America:* Mobile banking is now available from BOA. Check balances, pay bills, transfer money, and locate BOA ATMs and banking centers.
- *Kayak:* Kayak.com's branded app lets you easily search for flights, hotels, and car rentals. Includes trip itinerary and flight tracker information.
- *Netflix:* Part of your existing unlimited membership, you can get Netflix on your iPad, iPhone, or iPod Touch. Instantly watch TV and movies streaming from Netflix.
- *Travelocity:* The application lets you check flight and hotel information from your mobile phone. You can check flight status, airline schedules, and airport delay information from the FAA. The application also grabs your GPS coordinates to find local hotels, and lets you read reviews, check room rates, and even make a reservation from your handset.
- *Virtual Zippo Lighter:* This realistic virtual lighter sways with you as you move, and even reacts when you try to blow it out. You can choose from several different lighter images or customize your own.

Productivity Apps

- *Evernote:* This app allows you to take notes on a variety of devices, and then stores all of them for you in one location in the cloud. In other words, you can store photos, notes, and documents generated on a variety of devices, all on your Evernote account located in cyberspace.

◆ *Instapaper:* Through Instapaper you can save web articles you browsed on your iPhone for later reading, using a browser bookmarklet. The Instapaper website reformats your saved articles (sans Flash ads and clutter) for quick reading on the desktop.

◆ *Yammer:* Yammer brings together all of a company's employees inside a private, secure enterprise social network. This enterprise platform lets businesses set up a Twitter-like service, allowing for the open exchange of ideas, links, and documents within enterprise communities.

Financial Tools

◆ *Bloomberg Mobile:* Use this app when you're on the go to access financial news, stock quotes, company descriptions, market leaders and laggers, price charts, market-trends analysis, customized lists of stocks, and more.

◆ *CNNMoney:* With breaking business stories and complete in-depth market coverage in a customizable format, CNNMoney provides real-time reporting of financial news and analysis, as well as data and charts.

◆ *iStockManager:* For continuous access to, and control over, your TD Ameritrade account, use iStockManager. You can get equity and option trading, streaming data, real-time balances and positions, news, and more on your mobile device.

Organizers/Time Savers

◆ *Barcode Scanner:* Barcode Scanner handles bar codes— including 2D/QR codes—and lets you look up the associated product or URL for instant price checks and comparison shopping.

◆ *Craigsphone:* Search and browse Craigslist posts that were generated near your current GPS location with Craigsphone. The app also has tools for posting your own listings with photos and maps.

Utilities

◆ *AntiDroidTheft:* If you lose your phone, AntiDroidTheft turns on remote GPS tracking so that you can determine its location. You can also trigger the phone's camera to shoot an image that might help you locate the handset.

◆ *Gas Buddy:* Locates the most affordable gas station closest to your present location in both the United States and Canada. Includes maps and a "price freshness" guide to let you know when prices were last updated.

◆ *HubSpot Website Grader:* Interested in finding out how your mobile website (and your regular website) stacks up against the competition? This incredible free tool from HubSpot analyzes how effective your website is at generating traffic, inbound links, and leads. It's an indispensable tool for anyone who runs or owns a mobile or traditional website.

◆ *Photoshop.com:* Adobe's Photoshop.com mobile gives you an arsenal of tools to use on your Android phone. You can crop, rotate, color-correct, or change images to black-and-white with a beautifully intuitive interface.

◆ *Wi-Fi Analyzer:* Want to find the least-crowded WiFi channel? Wi-Fi Analyzer shows a graphical representation of WiFi SSID signal strength, plus which channels are being used.

◆ *Wi-Fi Finder:* A must-have for travelers, Wi-Fi Finder is a directory of paid and free WiFi hotspots in more than 280,000 locations in 140 countries. You can filter results by provider or by location (restaurant, café, and so on).

■■■

We've covered a lot of ground in this chapter. We started by discussing the different mobile operating systems and their market share around the globe. Then we touched on mobile carriers and manufacturers. We wrapped up by explaining why businesses invest in apps, and what the top mobile apps are.

We still have a lot to cover, but by reviewing these foundational elements, you're ready to learn about mobile marketing strategy and integration.

Ready?

Do This:

◆ Familiarize yourself with the various mobile operating systems. Borrow your friends' phones and learn how to use Android, iOS, Windows, and other operating systems.

◆ The next time you're visiting an AT&T, Verizon, or Sprint store, ask for a quick tour of the manufacturers' handsets. Figure out which ones provide the best phones.

◆ Download several of the apps listed in this chapter. More important, use them! Remember, you can't understand mobile media if you don't use mobile media.

Don't Do This:

◆ Don't assume that just because you've read about mobile marketing, you understand it completely. The best way to genuinely understand it is to experience it. Don't be shy; press some buttons or icons on your phone and see where it takes you!

Note

1. www.billshrink.com/cell-phones/carrier-compare/index.html; accessed October 24, 2011.

Chapter 9

Thinking Strategically about Your Mobile Marketing Campaign

The growing importance of mobile marketing has made developing a mobile strategy almost a prerequisite for a successful campaign. Keep in mind, one of the reasons you're reading this book is to learn how to grow your business with mobile marketing. Simply sending out mass text messages to customers won't act as a silver bullet to increase revenue. To ensure your mobile marketing practices grow effectively, you'll need to properly design, plan, and implement a mobile marketing campaign that meets your strategic objectives.

Let's begin by reviewing a couple of important concepts before we get started on planning your mobile marketing campaign:

Mobile marketing involves connecting and communicating with the consumer (B2C market) or customer (B2B market) via mobile devices such as cellular phones, smartphones, and tablets. The purpose of your mobile marketing campaign may be to send a simple marketing message, offer new products and services, send users to a mobile website, or ask for feedback in the form of simple surveys or polls. These purposes can be accomplished by using some of the following methods:

- ◆ *SMS or MMS:* Send text messages or multimedia messages to customers to inform them of special offers, new product releases, and other information.

- *Mobile display ads:* Use mobile banner ads to send customers to a website specifically designed to be viewed on a mobile device.
- *Social media:* Tap into services like Twitter, Facebook, and Google+ to share content with mobile customers.
- *Mobile paid search:* Use Google, Bing, or Yahoo! to drive prospects to your mobile landing page.
- *Location-based marketing:* Connect with prospects and customers via location-based services, near field communications, Bluetooth, or location-based advertising.
- *Mobile applications:* Feature apps that can be downloaded and installed from an application store (such as the iOS App Store or Android Marketplace), and that customers can use to build interest in a product or learn more.

Benefits of Mobile Marketing

To understand the benefits of mobile marketing, it's a good idea to explore the unique ways consumers use mobile devices as the "connective tissue" between marketers' online and offline consumer touch points. Here are several ways mobile devices are different from other forms of marketing communication methods:

- The mobile device is personal and rarely shared with another person.
- The mobile device is always carried by the consumer.
- The mobile device is always turned on.
- The mobile device has a built-in payment system.
- The mobile device allows for accurate audience measurement.
- The mobile device captures the social element of media consumption.
- The mobile device has a physical presence in a specific location.

Tracking the effectiveness of mobile marketing campaigns is easier than doing so for traditional programs. It's a simple process to follow an individual with a unique phone number attached to every action; plus, you can instantly communicate with your audience.

Your audience is most likely carrying their mobile devices with them, which means they can always receive messages. This is superior to other forms of marketing, whereby the audience has to be in a specific place to see a billboard or view an advertisement.

Marketing through mobile devices is also very efficient. Producing content for mobile view, such as audio or video, is very inexpensive when compared to producing content for desktop computers. However, the smaller screen sizes, lower resolution, and lower data transfer rates on mobile devices mean the content has to be simpler in design and execution.

Imagine the efficiencies of mobile marketing to customers who always have with them promotional coupons, vouchers, and other incentives, because the incentives are sent as part of a mobile campaign. For example, customers who receive a text message coupon offering them 20 percent off a food item at a restaurant are more likely to bring their mobile phones with them to the restaurant and actually use the coupon than customers who have to clip something out of a newspaper.

Disadvantages of Mobile Marketing

As just detailed, mobile marketing has many benefits, but we'd be remiss if we didn't also alert you to its disadvantages. Here they are:

- ◆ *Difficult navigation:* True, smartphones today are better at navigating the Internet than other mobile devices in the past, but navigating online is still more cumbersome on a mobile device than on a PC. That's why it's so important to design your mobile content so that it can be easily navigated on a device without a standard mouse and keyboard.
- ◆ *Differing operating systems:* As noted in Chapter 8, the two most popular operating systems in use on mobile devices today are iOS and Android. Both behave and display content differently, so make sure you test your content on every OS your customers will likely be using.
- ◆ *Privacy:* Customers are very attached to their mobile devices and you have to respect their use preferences, so you need to

give very clear instructions for opting out of marketing you send them.

You will experience other advantages and disadvantages as you develop and test your mobile marketing strategy, but for now be aware of the ones listed here as we move forward to developing a mobile marketing campaign.

How to Develop a Mobile Marketing Campaign

Now that you have the essential background information about mobile marketing in mind, you're ready to start thinking about planning your own mobile strategy. Here are the steps to creating and developing an effective mobile marketing campaign.

Do Background Planning

When starting any marketing campaign, you should begin by asking the following questions:

- What is the objective of this campaign?
- Who is your target audience?
- How long will this campaign run?
- Are you using other media to support or supplement your mobile media plan?

Define Your Objectives

What do you want your campaign to accomplish? Are you trying to increase awareness of your company, boost sales of a certain product or service, establish your branding, or something else? Clearly identify what it is you want to accomplish with your campaign before moving forward with further planning.

Identify Your Target Audience

Immediately after defining the objective(s) of your marketing strategy, you should identify your primary target audience. This will help to ensure that you tailor all elements of the marketing strategy specifically to this audience, enabling you to communicate with these customers as effectively as possible.

A good way to identify a target audience is to create a profile of a sample member of this group. Answer the following questions to get started:

1. Who would have a need for the specific product or service you are trying to market?
2. What is the ideal, manageable size of your primary target audience? Avoid being either too specific (e.g., "31-year-old male businessmen living in Manhattan") or too vague (e.g., "teenagers") to find an audience that is the right scope for your campaign.
3. Which methods of communication would work well in connecting with this audience? Look at demographic information about which age groups and types of people use mobile devices, and how they use them.

Different groups of people respond variously to what they see and read. Their tastes and preferences will affect how well they respond to the type of communications they receive, so make sure to research your target audience thoroughly before making other plans.

DEVISE CAMPAIGN STRATEGIES

Now that you have clearly defined your objectives and identified your target audience, you can start planning campaign strategies. Even though you are planning a mobile marketing campaign, you should decide which methods of mobile communication you want to use (audio? video? mobile websites?). You should also choose whether you want to *push* information to customers, or *pull* them to your company to start a dialog.

Push-based campaigns mean you send information out to customers and hope they respond by purchasing your product or service. Push can include sending text messages to everyone on a mailing list or informing him or her of, say, an album release or new promotion.

Pull and dialogue-based campaigns will require more planning and effort, but they also tend to be more effective at turning potential buyers into actual sales. Pull-based campaigns focus on "pulling" customers back to your company, such as by using SMS to send out a link to your website, or building an application customers can download, which will inform them about your product.

There are several other factors to consider when you're in the strategic planning stage of a campaign. Is your campaign intended to be brand-oriented or promotion-oriented? A brand campaign is designed to create a connection with your customer over the long term. A promotion campaign is designed to give your customer a reason to buy your product or service immediately.

The diagram in Figure 9.1 illustrates how several different kinds of companies might explore the nature of their campaigns. The Y-axis indicates whether the campaign is brand-oriented or promotion-oriented. The X-axis indicates whether the campaign is location-centric or nonlocation-centric. For example, if your company is a brick-and-mortar retailer, your campaign will be location-centric,

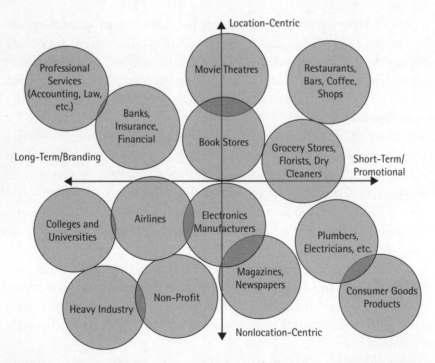

FIGURE 9.1   As you're developing your mobile marketing strategy, decide whether you need a brand-oriented or promotion-oriented campaign. You'll also want to consider whether your campaign should be location-centric or nonlocation-centric.
Source: Dr. Reshma Shah and Jamie Turner

because you want to drive people to your location. If you're a non-profit organization, your campaign won't be location-centric, because you don't usually need to drive people to a specific brick-and-mortar location.

Determine Length of Campaign

Once you've specified strategies for your mobile campaign, the next step is to decide how long it will run. Will your campaign be a one-shot action, or will it be a series of actions? The length and duration of the campaign will affect how you design it. If you want this campaign to run for an extended length of time, be sure to repeatedly "inject" it with advertising activity. Otherwise, customer response will slow to a halt.

INCORPORATE OTHER MEDIA

Finally, determine what other media you will be using to promote your mobile marketing strategy. Are you going to inform customers about a mobile application through e-mail and web advertising? Will you tell people to sign up for text message updates through radio commercials? How you use other media should have a profound effect on how you design your campaign. Likewise, your campaign objectives and your target audience should affect your selection of the types of other media you will use.

■■■

The preceding are basic considerations, and may even seem obvious, depending on your marketing background, but they are worth addressing here because they are so important. Without clearly defined answers to these preliminary questions and considerations, your mobile marketing campaign won't set off in the direction it should, to succeed.

Budgeting and Scheduling

Now that the preliminary background planning phase is complete, you're ready to move on to budgeting and scheduling. Ask these questions to help you determine the budget you'll need to produce your campaign, and how to schedule it:

- ◆ When do you need the campaign to start?
- ◆ How much money do you intend to spend on mobile media?
- ◆ How much do you intend to spend on other forms of media?
- ◆ How many messages are you planning to send?

SET THE START DATE

Choose a date you want the campaign to start and work backwards from there to draft a preliminary schedule. For example, if you want your campaign to start on June 8, and you need to have advertising materials ready to deliver a week in advance, set the deadline for advertising material to June 1. Work backwards in this way for all campaign components until you have established all the dates for your campaign. Don't forget to include the dates for other forms of media (if you are using them).

ASSESS THE COST OF MOBILE MEDIA

There are several cost considerations to make when planning mobile media for your campaign. Creative, promotion, and messages all have their own costs. How much will it cost to set up a mobile website or to develop a mobile application? Determine these line items before moving forward.

CALCULATE THE COST OF OTHER MEDIA

If you are incorporating other media into your mobile marketing campaign (such as print ads, Internet ads, radio, etc.), factor in those costs as well. Mass media is very expensive. Make sure supporting your mobile media campaign with other media is worth what you'll have to pay to do so.

DETERMINE THE NUMBER OF MESSAGES

Finally, determine how many messages you intend to send as part of your campaign. This will depend on your campaign strategy, as discussed earlier. Are you focusing on a push, pull, or dialog-based campaign? Deciding that will help you figure how many messages you need to send and how frequently you need to send them. Note that the cost per message decreases the more you send. For example, the cost per message to send 5,000 messages might be $0.055 per message; but if you send 20,000, that cost would drop to $0.035 per message.

After you have lined up your budget and schedule, you can begin planning the actual message of the campaign.

Content and Production

With the background information, budgeting, and scheduling completed, and with a good idea of the scale of your campaign in mind, you can start planning the types of message(s) you will send. It's important to wait until this phase to plan the details of your message so you can accurately assess whether to deliver it all at once or in waves, whether you want to target it to a large or small audience, and other considerations.

Answer these questions to help direct you as plan the content and production of your campaign message:

* What kind of message do you want to use in this campaign?
* How will you distribute your messages?
* Who will produce the message content or mobile application?
* Who will test the campaign?

Choose Message Type

Decide on the type of message you will use as part of your mobile marketing strategy. Will you send out SMS? Mobile display ads? A mobile application? Examine your target audience and background information before deciding on the method(s) of communication that would be most effective for connecting with your customers.

Make sure to consider the strengths and limitations of each type of message. For example, SMS messages are inexpensive, and are read by customers almost 100 percent of the time, but they are limited to 160 characters. Examine the benefits and drawbacks of each method of communication.

DECIDE ON DISTRIBUTION

Decide who will provide the platform necessary to implement your campaign. Are you going to do everything in-house, or will you outsource the implementation of your campaign to another firm? Look at your resources, with particular focus on the time frame and skills of your marketing team, to determine whether it would be more cost-effective to do it yourself or to have someone else take care of it.

Choose a Production Strategy

Once you've decided who will distribute and implement your campaign, you next need to choose how you will produce the messages you send out. If you are using a mobile application, will you produce it in-house, or will you hire an outside group to develop it? Who will design the SMS campaign or mobile website? Again, evaluate all your resources before making this decision.

CONDUCT TESTING

Testing your campaign is probably the most important step. Simply put, all of your other planning will be wasted if your campaign doesn't work. You must leave sufficient time to conduct exhaustive testing before launch, to work out the bugs in the technology. You must test each and every aspect of your mobile campaign (SMS, mobile application, mobile website, etc.).

■ ■ ■

After you've taken these steps, you are ready to move on to the final stages of planning for your mobile campaign.

Other Considerations

At this juncture, you understand essential background information about mobile marketing, you've established a budget and schedule, and have taken care of content and production. Now you're ready to plan the final elements of your campaign.

Here are three questions to answer before you enter this final phase:

- Who will organize and coordinate multiple media implementation?
- Where will you get your customer contacts?
- What will be measured?

COORDINATE MULTIPLE MEDIA IMPLEMENTATION

If you are going to use multiple forms of media, decide who will coordinate how your media works together. Have the activities for other media been properly planned? If your mobile marketing campaign relies heavily on other media forms to support it, it's very important to make sure this has been addressed.

COLLECT CUSTOMER INFO

If you plan on using SMS or other push methods to communicate with customers, how will you get their information? In the United States, selling opt-in lists is prohibited by law, so how else can you collect customer information? You might consider directing customers to a website where they can sign up for updates, or provide a phone number where they can text a keyword to sign up.

TAKE MEASUREMENTS

Another very important part of any marketing campaign is to determine how you will measure the success of your campaign. Many metrics are available for mobile marketing, such as number of messages sent, number of messages actually delivered, number of "stop" messages, number of customers who follow through with a message, and others. Establish the metrics you will you so you can evaluate accurately how effective your campaign is.

Why Think Strategically?

Mobile marketing can be very effective, for three important reasons: (1) It lets you connect with customers through a medium that is always on; (2) it is always available; and (3) it is very personal. Moreover, a mobile marketing strategy can easily implement other forms of communication and media to reach a target audience and turn prospective customers into sales. Today, almost every man, woman, and child has his or her own personal mobile device, making it easier than ever before to reach both current customers and new prospects. Why not implement a mobile strategy for your next marketing campaign? See how effective using this new technology to reach customers can be.

Do This:
- Treat mobile as a channel by testing mobile-specific features such as SMS messaging, applications, or location-based services.
- Use mobile as connective tissue, with the potential to link the online and offline consumer experiences with brands. Michael Becker, managing director of the Mobile Marketing Association, uses the expression "connective tissue" to describe the capability of mobile to become an indispensable, fully integrated part of marketing and business overall.

Don't Do This:
- Don't name an internal owner of the mobile channel. Without a designated in-house mobile expert, a mobile strategy will not be effective.
- Don't place mobile in a silo, where it may be left out of the overall marketing strategy. Communicating cross-functionally (not just with the marketing team) and cross-company is crucial to achieving long-term success with mobile.

Part III

Taking a Deeper Dive into Mobile Marketing Tools Pool

Chapter 10

How to Set Up a Mobile Website

If you're like a lot of businesspeople, your mobile website is either nonexistent or not as good as you'd like it to be. If either of those is the case for you, you've come to the right chapter, because here we're going to talk about how to design, create, and launch a mobile website. Then we're going to explain how to drive traffic to your mobile website. After all, what's the point of having a mobile website if nobody stops by for a visit, right?

The first step to developing a mobile website is to get inside the mind of your customer. When you step outside yourself and go inside the mind of your customers, you begin to see things from their perspective. The result is that you'll be able to design the site from a user-experience point of view rather than from a company-centric point of view. Furthermore, by designing from the user-experience side of the equation, you'll deepen your customer engagement and encourage repeat visits.

Typically, given the medium, your mobile website will be more streamlined than your corporate website. People who will be visiting your mobile site are themselves *mobile*, and they have a very specific set of needs—none of which include the desire to read a lot of extraneous information. Thus, you can do without company press releases, employee bios, case studies, company philosophy, and photos of your employee holiday party.

Simply put, you'll want to keep your mobile site simple. For the most part, that means designing it to comprise only 5 to 10 pages. Only in rare cases would you want a mobile site with more than 10 pages on it.

Enough with the generalities; let's get down to specifics. Let's drill down and take a closer look at some specific businesses and analyze their customers, to demonstrate how you can then figure out what might be going on inside your own customers' heads when they visit your mobile site.

Getting Inside the Mind of Your Customer

Dr. Flint McGlaughlin, the CEO of MECLABS, an Internet optimization laboratory, says that the trick to designing effective marketing campaigns isn't to optimize your web pages; it's to *optimize your customer's thought sequences* instead.

When visitors go to a mobile (or regular) website, their mind follows a specific series of steps, depending on their particular situation.

Voice Search and Its Potential Impact on Your Business

More and more people are using voice search to conduct searches from their mobile devices. This is important to keep in mind if you're just starting up and haven't named your company yet. If, say, you name your catering business "90-Second Catering," it may come up as "92nd Catering" from a mobile voice search, which will frustrate potential customers.

Let's explore the mind-set and the thought processes of a variety of people who are searching the web using their mobile devices for various companies. Note that the list here is not comprehensive, but by reviewing the different company types we do cover, and how customers engage with mobile websites to reach them, you'll get a good sense of why it's so important to get inside the mind of your customer *before* you develop your site.

Restaurants, Bars, and Coffee Shops

There are two kinds of prospects here: those who are searching for a *specific* restaurant, bar, or coffee shop, and those who are searching for *any* restaurant, bar, or coffee shop.

In the first case, the prospects or customers have probably used Google, Bing, or Yahoo! from their mobile devices to look up your business. Once they've clicked through to your mobile site, they're interested in one of five things (in order of importance): your location (with a mobile-friendly map), your menu (with prices), your hours of operation, your phone number, and, possibly, whether or not you have WiFi.

In the second case, when people are looking for *any* restaurant, bar, or coffee shop, they're interested in the same five things; but you might want to include a "hook" or a promotion that says something like, "One free dessert for any group that presents this mobile coupon."

The key point here is to set up your mobile site so that it appeals to both kinds of customers. By doing so, you'll be able to draw them into your mobile site and, as a result, lure them to your location.

Brick-and-Mortar Retailers

For these kinds of companies, your prospect's thought process probably goes something like this: (1) Does this company have the product I'm looking for? (2) If so, where is the nearest location? (3) What are the store's hours of operation?

Some prospects might also be looking for coupons, so including a "daily deal" link is a great way to drive foot traffic to your location. Also, remember that people might actually want to buy products via their mobile devices, so if e-commerce capabilities are part of your regular website, you might want to include them on your mobile site, too.

Airlines, Railways, and Other Transportation Services

Imagine you're in your car and have found your airline's website on your mobile device. What's the first thing you're probably interested in checking? Whether or not your flight is on time, delayed, or cancelled. The second thing you might want to do is to check in via your mobile device so you don't have to stand in line at the airport. Those two items are probably followed quickly by concerns related to flight schedules, baggage, and booking future flights.

Law Firms, Accounting Firms, and Other Professional Service Firms

One of the main reasons someone would visit a professional service firm's mobile website is because he or she is trying to find the location of your office, so be sure you include an easy link to a map, as well as a click-to-call button so the person can phone the front desk. (Keep in mind, sometimes, new customers may be lost in the lobby of a building or courtyard, where a map isn't as helpful as a friendly receptionist.)

When designing a mobile site for a professional services firm, remember that a clean, uncluttered look with a lot of white space gives visitors a sense that your company is first class. Resist the temptation to use too much color; and, by all means, err on the side of classic rather than contemporary. That said, if your business in an ad agency, interior design firm, digital agency, or some other creative profession, it's fine to go contemporary. But if you're a law firm, accounting firm, or financial services firm, stick with a classic design.

Nonprofit Organizations

There are three kinds of people who visit a nonprofit organization's mobile site: those who want to donate, those who want to receive help, and those who want to find out what the group has been up to.

It's possible to accommodate all three kinds of visitors on one site. One approach is to install a large "Donate Here" button, in red, on the upper right-hand side of the site, and below, provide clean, minimalist links to other sections of the site. Remember, one of the quickest ways to deliver information to people about your cause is to show a photograph, so don't shy away from a colorful image that quickly tells a story. (While we discourage loading your mobile site with too many bandwidth-clogging photographs, an occasional photograph that's strategically placed can go a long way toward telling your story.)

Hotels, Spas, and Other Hospitality Organizations

If you're in the hospitality industry, most of your customers are interested in finding a hotel, booking a room, or cancelling a reservation. They're also interested in talking to someone (it's not called the hospitality industry for nothing). Make it easy for them: Feature large, simple, easy-to-see buttons, front and center, on the site. And make sure a click-to-call button is one of the first things they see; many people need special attention because, for example, they've left their cell phone in their room or need to discuss handicap access at a specific location.

Colleges, Universities, and Other Educational Institutions

There are two kinds of visitors to a college/university mobile site: students who are lost, and potential students who want more information. That's not to say that there aren't other items of interest; for example, entrance requirements and fees/tuition. But the primary users of a mobile site for an educational institution will be lost students and potential students.

Banks, Credit Unions, and Other Financial Institutions

For banks and credit unions, it's all about the ATM locations, the branch locations, and, possibly, mobile banking. For other financial institutions, it's about quick access to financial information.

Other Businesses

There are thousands of different kinds of businesses, and we can't cover all of them, but you get the idea: The starting point for designing any mobile website is to *get inside the mind of your customer and work backwards from there.*

Once you reverse your thinking and start seeing things from your customer's point of view, it will be easy to track the logical flow of setting up and designing your mobile website.

With that in mind, let's do a quick recap of how to begin the process of designing your mobile website. We'll cover some of the items already mentioned, plus introduce a few new ideas, like designing for speed and for multiple devices.

Ready? Here goes:

1. *Get inside the mind of your customers.* As stated, the first step for any successful marketing program is to get inside the mind of your customers. Think about your mobile site from their perspective. Where do they tend to be when they access your website from their mobile devices? What information are they likely to be looking for? What's the easiest way to provide them that information?

2. *Analyze your customers' thought sequences.* When you analyze your customers' thought sequences, you're thinking through the steps they take to gather information and process it. You may find that several different kinds of customers visit your mobile site, and that each of them has slightly different thought patterns. You can still design one site around multiple thought sequences, as long as you provide a simple, logical flow of information for each kind of customer.

3. *Keep to a minimum the number of design elements.* Resist the temptation to cram your mobile site with tons of information. Don't think like someone who is writing a brochure. Instead, think in terms of writing a text message. Be brief. And don't include any design element unless it absolutely has to be there.

4. *Design for speed.* Pages load slower on a mobile site than they do on a typical computer. Consequently, abandon rates tend to be much higher. Make sure your web designer does everything he or she can to streamline the site. Avoid using Flash and video on your mobile site home page. Use JPEGs and GIFs instead.

5. *Design for multiple devices.* Right now, there are no standards for all mobile devices, so you'll have to design your site based on the top four or five handsets and screens used by your customers. This means your site won't always render perfectly for every single visitor, but at this stage of the game, the best you can do is to design for the majority of customers based on their handset choices.

The Nuts and Bolts of Mobile Web Design

It's time to get specific about the technical issues you'll confront when designing a mobile website. In an earlier chapter, we discussed the three different approaches you can take when creating a mobile website. Here's a quick recap:

♦ *Automated systems:* These systems use software tools to read the code in your existing website and translate it into a mobile-friendly version. As mentioned earlier, this is not the best route to take since these automated systems simply repackage your site without careful consideration of the nuances of design. Tread lightly if you're thinking of going down this path.

♦ *Plug-and-play systems:* There are several good companies offering plug-and-play systems that allow you to create a mobile website with varying degrees of control. These companies include: Mobify, Wirenode, Mippin Mobilizer, Onbile, MoFuse, and HubSpot. If your website has been designed using WordPress or Drupal, there are several free plug-ins you can use to create mobile versions of your site, too.

♦ *Third-party agencies or design firms:* If customization is critical to you, you'll want to work with an agency or web design firm. It'll cost significantly more than the plug-and-play solutions, but you'll have much greater control over branding elements, search engine optimization, website analytics, and other features that may make this route your best option.

Mobile Browser Redirect Tool

If you're looking for a simple way to create browser redirect code for your mobile site, Mobile Moxie has an easy-to-use tool that's readily available. Just visit MobileMoxie.com and search for the browser redirection tool. Follow the instructions and, before you know it, you'll have the code you need.

If you decide to go with the third option, to hire an agency or design firm to create your mobile site, there's a relatively easy approach to take. Essentially, you'll want the agency to include a line of code for your home page that "sniffs out" the screen size of the browser (or visitor) trying to access your site. If the visitor is arriving from a web browser that's smaller than 600 pixels wide, then it's almost certain that person is using a mobile device.

When that's the case, the visitor will be redirected to your mobile site, which can "sit" outside your regular site (if you're using some of the plug-and-play systems), or inside your site (if your agency or web design firm is designing the site).

The Language of the Internet

There are a few terms you'll need defined before you go much further into the development of your mobile site. This knowledge will come in handy even after you've built your site, because these are terms used frequently in meetings and conversations.

- ◆ *Uniform Resource Locator (URL):* Another name for the address of a website. An example of a URL is www.HubSpot .com or www.60SecondMarketer.com.
- ◆ *Domain name:* The part of your site's URL that includes the letters before the dot. HubSpot and 60SecondMarketer are two examples of domain names.
- ◆ *Domain extension:* The part of your site address that includes the letters *after* the dot. For example, com, org, mobi, and edu are domain extensions.
- ◆ *Subdomain:* The part of your site address that appears *before* the domain name. For example, www.m.ABC.com is a sub-domain for ABC.com.
- ◆ *Subdirectory:* The part of your site address that comes *after* the domain extension. For example, www.ABC.com/mobile is a subdirectory for ABC.com.

These terms are shown graphically in Figure 10.1.

Some businesses choose to build their mobile websites as separate entities from their regular websites. For example, a company called Green Widgets might have its regular site at www.Green-Widgets.com and its mobile site at www.GreenWidgets.mobi. If the

FIGURE 10.1   You probably won't have to spend too much time worrying about protocols, subdomains, and subdirectories. Even so, it never hurts to understand the anatomy of a URL.

sniffer code in the company's regular site figures out that the visitor is coming from a mobile device, he or she will be redirected to the mobile site at www.GreenWidgets.mobi.

Alternatively, you can build your mobile site within your existing site. This can be done by creating a subdomain like www.m.Green-Widgets.com or a subdirectory like www.GreenWidgets.com/mobile. Again, once the sniffer code in the regular site figures out the device the visitor is using, he or she will be redirected either to the mobile subdomain at www.m.GreenWidgets.com or the subdirectory at www.GreenWidgets.com/mobile.

All of these options are fine, but we've found it simplest to create a subdirectory and redirect visitors to that subdirectory. When a mobile version of your site is included in a subdirectory, it's much easier to manage because the entire mobile site simply sits within your website. Plus, mobile search engines do a better job of ranking your mobile site, because the m. subdirectory lets them know that it's been set up specifically for mobile.

Resources for Mobile Website Development

As you're developing your mobile website, there are several tools and resources you'll want to access during the development process. These tools can help you understand mobile users, and can even provide you with mobile emulators to test your site on.

- ◆ *Comscore.com and Nielsen.com:* Both these companies provide research into mobile usage. They even deliver a monthly record of the top handsets in use throughout the United States and Europe.
- ◆ *AdMob.com, MillennialMedia.com, GetJar.com, and Netbiscuits .com:* These advertising networks have plenty of research and

data available on mobile phone usage, including free reports on the top mobile handsets in use around the globe.

◆ *MobileMoxie.com, DeviceAnywhere.com, and MobiReady.com:* You can test your site with each of these tools, which deliver evaluations on how you can improve your website's functionality.

We've discussed a number of important topics in this chapter, including how to design a mobile website from your customer's perspective; how to build a site using automated systems, plug-and-play systems, or web design firms; how to interpret the language of the Internet; and how to use outside resources to conduct additional research and test your site.

In the next chapter, we're going to discuss how to use Short Message Service (SMS) and Multimedia Message Service (MMS) to drive more customers to your business.

Do This:

◆ Get inside the mind of your customers. By doing so, you'll be able to design your site to suit their particular needs.
◆ Design your mobile site for speed and functionality. By streamlining the site, you'll improve the customer experience.
◆ Test your site as it's in development. This means using the site emulators mentioned in this chapter, as well as "live" prospects and customers to test the site's functionality and user-friendliness.

Don't Do This:

◆ Don't assume that your site will work on every device. As time goes on, the standards for mobile site development will work themselves out, but for now, it's impossible to design a site that works on 100 percent of the available handsets.
◆ Don't use an automated system to create a mobile website. Instead, rely on the plug-and-play or third-party options outlined in this chapter.

Chapter 11

Using SMS and MMS to Drive Customers to Your Business

Let's kick off this chapter by focusing on Short Message Service (SMS), which will lay a good foundation for the discussion about Multimedia Message Service (MMS) later in the chapter.

Of all the mobile marketing tools at your disposal, SMS is the one you're probably most familiar with. Recall from Chapter 2 that the American Red Cross used SMS for its highly successful Haiti relief campaign. FedEx and UPS send alerts to customers via text regarding delivery updates on their packages. And, of course, if you have a teenager, you are no doubt aware that texting is the number one form of communication for kids between the ages of 12 and 17.

SMS was originally conceived in the 1980s, but the first commercial text message wasn't sent until December 3, 1992, from a young engineer at Airwide Solutions.[1] The message ("Happy Christmas") opened the door to some fundamental changes in the way people connect with one another.

There are several reasons why SMS has been, and continues to be, successful for businesses:

- Text messages are read within 4 minutes of receipt, as opposed to 48 hours for e-mail.[2]
- Virtually every smartphone has SMS capabilities.

- ◆ Consumers are very familiar with the medium (4 billion texts are sent daily, compared to 2.9 billion Google searches made daily).[3]
- ◆ SMS is relatively inexpensive.
- ◆ SMS is easily scalable.
- ◆ The data from an SMS campaign is easy to track, making ROI calculations a piece of cake.

Facts and Figures about SMS

The Pew Internet & American Life Project reports that teenagers in the United States contact peers daily using text more than any other communication channel (54 percent). This includes making phone calls (38 percent), talking face to face (33 percent), and using e-mail (11 percent). And it's not just teens that are using SMS. A recent study by Merkle found that 63 percent of adults aged 30 to 39 in the United States, text; and 49 percent of adults 40 to 49. What's more, 26 percent of U.S. adults have opted in to receive messages on their mobile devices from an average of three companies sending them mobile messages monthly.[4]

Clearly, SMS ain't going away anytime soon.

All that said, there are a number of concerns to address before using SMS to market to customers. For starters, many consumers are worried about receiving spam via SMS. And they're worried about how the data collected via SMS will be used by the companies they've connected with. Finally, some highly publicized abuses of SMS by less-than-legitimate organizations, have made some consumers reluctant to fully embrace the technology.

It's also important to remember that SMS is just one tool in your mobile marketing tool chest. And it's not one that performs optimally in isolation. If you're going to use SMS, be sure to incorporate it as part of a broader mix of techniques you're implementing to engage customers.

How to Use SMS to Connect with Customers

The use of SMS is limited only by your imagination—this is a medium that makes it easy to be creative. Another big advantage is that it doesn't cost a lot of money to implement.

With that in mind, take a look at some of the creative ways companies and professionals are using SMS to connect with customers and grow their revenues:

- *CNN, Mashable, and ABC News* send out push notifications via SMS, alerting subscribers to important news and information. The full stories are available on their apps and mobile websites.

- *Doctors and dentists* are using SMS to remind patients about upcoming appointments. Patients can confirm their appointments, thereby reducing the number of no-shows and thus increasing revenues for the doctors in the process.

- *Real estate agents* are using SMS to provide property information to prospective buyers. Interested parties can learn more about a listing by texting a specific ID number on the sign, enabling them to receive detailed information quickly.

- *Gas stations* are using text messages to alert customers when gas prices are scheduled to increase.

- *Trade shows and other events* are using text messages to alert attendees about special promotions on- and off-site. They're also being used for text-to-vote polls, which allow attendees to see the results during presentations.

- *Symantec* provides text alerts to subscribers via its Workflow solution. The company sends out alerts to subscribers who need to be notified when a new computer virus breaks out on the Internet.

- *British Airways* and other airlines provide text alerts to travelers who want to be notified when a flight is delayed or cancelled.

- *Walgreen's in the United States and Lloyd's in the United Kingdom* both use SMS to alert customers when their prescriptions are filled. Other services send reminders to patients when it's time to take their medicines.

- *Blue Shield of California* is including text4baby as part of its Prenatal Education program, which provides expectant and new mothers information about prenatal and postpartum care.

- *Safaricom, in Kenya,* offers an SMS solution called M-PESA that allows customers to pay for goods and services using SMS. Users enter the amount they want to pay, enter their PINs, confirm the details, and press OK. The sales assistant sends a receipt for the transaction on the spot.
- *Marriott Hotels* offers a text alert to visitors who left items such as wallets, purses, or other luggage in their rooms. All visitors receive a "Thank You" text after their departure.
- *Colleges, universities, and high schools* are using SMS to send weather-related alerts and other emergency notifications. Messages can be sent to entire student bodies instantly.
- *Banks and other financial institutions* send text messages to customers who opt in to receive alerts when their balances are running low.
- *RentPayment, VacationRentPayment, and StorageRentPayment* provide ways for customers to pay rent via text. Once renters register, they can pay their bills via text, quickly and easily.
- *ArmenTel conducted an SMS contest* that prompted contestants to answer a series of questions, with each answer bringing them closer to a hidden "treasure." Over the 90-day campaign, more than 8,000 prizes were given away and more than 11 percent of ArmenTel's customers participated.[5]

How to Set Up, Launch, and Run an SMS Campaign

It's important to understand the requirements for an SMS campaign before you begin to create one. There's a 160-character limit for an SMS campaign, which means that your copy will have to be very concise and highly efficient in getting your point across. You'll also want to make sure you're complying with the rules about SMS, which can vary based on carrier.

There are five key elements to an SMS campaign that you'll want to keep in mind as you develop your program:

    1. Keyword: This is the word that users text in to the short code (described next). It needs to be memorable, easy to type, and relevant to your brand. It's typically eight characters or fewer. Consider a lot of options before settling on your keyword. You might even sleep on them overnight before making a final decision.

2. *Short code:* Users text the keyword to a five-digit code called the short code. For example, your ad or point-of-purchase poster might encourage users to text FREESTUFF (the keyword) to 12345 (the short code). One key decision on this front is whether you should use a dedicated (or branded) short code like COKE (for the Coca-Cola Company), or a shared short code like 54321. Shared codes are more cost-effective, but dedicated codes may be a worthwhile investment if yours is a large brand.

3. *Call to action (CTA):* The CTA comprises the keyword, the short code, and the benefit or value to the user. The challenge is to encourage action in just one sentence. Therefore, you'll also want to test your way to success. For example, you might want to compare the results of "Text KEYWORD to SHORTCODE for a free trial" against "Text KEYWORD to SHORTCODE for free audio books."

4. *Supporting media:* This encompasses the ad, poster, radio commercial, TV spot, and/or digital ad that encourage users to text the keyword. The choice of media type, placement, and creative will influence the success of your campaign even more than the keyword, short code, or, possibly, the CTA. For best results, make sure your SMS CTA is prominently displayed. And if you're running a TV spot, keep it on the screen as long as possible (better still, throughout the entire spot).

5. *Response:* After users respond, they should receive a message from you confirming receipt. This may be an opportunity to further differentiate your brand. For example, if you run a bar in Hawaii, responding with "Awesome, Dude" would be fine. And if you're a banker on Wall Street, using "Awesome, Dude" is perfectly fine, too. (We're kidding. Don't do that, bankers.)

The 14 Most Powerful Words in Marketing

Research indicates that consumers respond most readily to the following 14 words.[6] Be sure to use them in your calls to action:

- Free
- Now
- You
- Save
- Money
- Easy
- Guarantee

- Health
- Results
- New
- Love
- Discovery
- Proven
- Safety

Meet SMS's Attractive Cousin: MMS

We've spent a good amount of time talking about SMS and how it can be used to grow your sales and revenues. But let's not forget about Multimedia Message Service, which has all the power of SMS, *and* it features the capability to tell a story with images, sound, and full-motion video. You can even use MMS to write longer descriptions, which include links to mobile websites, because it doesn't have the 160-character limit of SMS.

Of the nearly 250 million people in the United States who send SMS messages, about 85 percent of them have the ability to send and receive MMS messages as well.[7] If you want to find out whether your customers can send and receive MMS messages, ask them if their mobile devices take pictures. If the answer is yes, chances are they have MMS-capable phones. You'll find that only a handful of phones in the United States today *can't* receive MMS.

What Can You Send via MMS?

Glad you asked. When you compare MMS to SMS, you'll find that MMS provides a lot more interesting options. Here's what you have to work with:

- *Images:* You can send images and integrate them directly into your customer's mobile phone inboxes. You can send images of your logo, a new product, or even a photograph of people interacting with your brand.

- ◆ *Text:* As mentioned, you don't have to worry about character restrictions with an MMS campaign. You can write several thousand words in your message (although most recipients won't read more than a few dozen). Better still, you can format the text in many ways, from adding color to changing fonts and styles.

- ◆ *Audio:* Are you selling an audio book? Are you in a band? Perhaps you're trying to encourage people to subscribe to your podcasts. If so, you'll want to include audio clips in your message, and MMS is perfect for that.

- ◆ *Animations:* These can range from animated icons, cartoon figures, or illustrations. Including animation is a great way to make your business stand out from its competitors.

- ◆ *Video:* Nearly all MMS phones can receive video files, so don't shy away from this powerful tool. If you use Final Cut Pro, iMovie, or QuickTime to encode your video, your message will be compatible with most mobile devices. Make sure, however, that your videos are no more than 15 frames per second and about 30 seconds in length, to ensure that your content will be delivered properly.

HOW TO RUN AN MMS CAMPAIGN

There are several approach options to choose from when it comes to running an MMS campaign. If you're a do-it-yourselfer, you might want to take a look at the applications offered by companies like Mogreet and CellySpace. Mogreet was founded by James Citron, a contributor to *Mobile Marketing For Dummies* (also published by John Wiley & Sons). And CellySpace, another well-respected company in the mobile marketing industry, provides a solid do-it-yourself foundation for anyone looking for online tools to help take advantage of SMS and MMS.

If you're not a do-it-yourselfer, you'll be better off working with an MMS service provider. And, certainly, if your campaign is large, complex, or requires customization, this is the way to go. Here are some of the benefits of working with an established MMS service provider: An MMS service provider can:

- *Manage the delivery of your content across multiple carriers and handsets.* That way, you don't have to worry about whether or not your MMS message will play on an Apple iPhone as well as it plays on a Samsung Focus.
- *Target subgroups of customers.* You'll find that the success of your campaigns improves the more you segment (or customize) the message. MMS service providers can help you do that.
- *Acquire short codes for you.* With an MMS service provider, you don't have to hassle with all the variables around a short code. Just give the provider a sense of what you're looking for, and its professionals will use their knowledge and expertise to get you the right one.
- *Track the success of your campaign.* What's the point of running a campaign if you're not tracking it? With the flood of data you can receive about your campaign, you'll want a company to analyze and draw insights from it. An MMS service provider can do that for you.
- *Manage carrier approval for you.* Carriers have a lot of rules and regulations around mobile marketing. Using an MMS service provider can help you navigate through those choppy waters.

Elements of an Opt-in Message for SMS and MMS Recipients

Tim Miller, president of SUMOTEXT, says there are five components of a compliant opt-in confirmation message:

1. The content provider's name
2. Description of the program
3. Intended frequency of alerts
4. Rate/cost disclosure (e.g., "Msg & Data rates may apply.")
5. Instructions on how to quit the service or get help

SMS and MMS Best Practices

Whether you're using SMS or MMS to provide product information, links to a mobile website, links to maps, click-to-call links, product videos, or any other form of communication, you'll want to follow these best practices:

◆ *Ask permission.* This is the biggie. If anyone ever comes to you with a list of "preapproved" names of people who "want to receive your messages on their mobile devices," just say no. They're selling spam (and not the good, tasty kind you'll find on your grocer's shelf). You must *always get opt-in consent* before messaging consumers. SMS and MMS messages can cost money, so it's important to let recipients know what they've opted in for prior to sending messages to them.

◆ *Offer something of value:* Mobile devices are very personal items, much more so than TVs, computers, or other technologies. Therefore, it's important to provide something of value to consumers who have opted in to receive messages from you. Never forget, they're giving up their data and some of their privacy when they connect with you via SMS or MMS, so reward them for their loyalty.

◆ *Use SMS and MMS for time-sensitive events.* American Idol used text messages to remind fans to tune into the program. Delta Air Lines uses SMS to keep travelers posted on flight schedules. Consumers respond positively to messages that provide information that makes their lives easier and more convenient.

In summary, SMS and MMS are good, solid tools that you can use to connect effectively and efficiently with customers and prospects. They may not be the newest tools in the mobile marketing kit, but when combined with other marketing media (like TV, outdoor, print, or radio), they can be very powerful indeed.

Do This:

◆ Before anything else, set goals and objectives for your campaign. What are you trying to accomplish? What's the desired outcome?

- ◆ Track your results. What's the point of running a mobile marketing campaign if you don't track the results? As they say, things that get measured improve.
- ◆ Integrate your campaign. You'll find your campaign gets the best results when it's integrated into a larger marketing program. One-offs don't work as well as long-term, integrated campaigns.

Don't Do This:

- ◆ Don't promote your SMS or MMS campaign where there's poor cell phone coverage. You can't further your cause on subways, inside some buildings, or other isolated areas.
- ◆ Don't expect instant results. The best mobile marketing campaigns build over the course of time. Sure, you'll want to see an initial "pop" when the campaign launches, but you'll find your best results come after running a consistent campaign.

Notes

1. www.160characters.org/news.php?action=view&nid=2471; accessed October 24, 2011.
2. Mobile Marketing Association, *Mobile Marketer's Classic Guide to Mobile Advertising, 3rd edition*, 2010, p. 43.
3. http://en.wikipedia.org/wiki/Text_messaging; accessed October 24, 2011.
4. Mobile Marketing Playbook, 360i, 2010, p. 28.
5. www.mmaglobal.com/studies/armentel-%E2%80%9Ctreasure-hunt%E2%80%9D-sms-contest-velti; accessed October 24, 2011.
6. Denny Hatch, Don Jackson, *2,239 Tested Secrets for Direct Marketing Success: The Pros Tell You Their Time-Proven Secrets* (New York: McGraw-Hill, 1998), p. 88.
7. http://mobithinking.com/mobile-marketing-tools/latest-mobile-stats; accessed October 24, 2011.

Chapter 12

How to Use Mobile Display Ads to Grow Your Sales and Revenue

We've covered a lot of ground in the preceding chapters. Beginning in Chapter 1, you learned how to dive right into mobile marketing. Since then, we've explored a number of mobile marketing tools and techniques. You also read about several highly successful mobile marketing case studies; and we've discussed how to use both SMS and MMS on your mobile websites.

Now it's time to delve into the wonderful world of mobile display advertising. To begin, a clarification: Don't confuse mobile display with mobile paid search, both of which we introduced in Chapter 5. Mobile paid search is another form of mobile advertising that's essentially paid search on a mobile device. Mobile display ads are the little banner ads you see on mobile websites, mobile apps, or even mobile games. (We cover mobile paid search in detail in the next chapter.)

According to Borrell Associates, mobile display ad spending in the United States will grow from $305 million in 2010 to $685 million in 2011 and to more than $8 billion by 2015, with $1.2 billion of that coming from *local advertisers*.[1] We've said this before, but it's worth repeating here, mobile marketing is ideal for local businesses, since most people who interact with a mobile marketing campaign are, themselves, *mobile* and are looking to buy something in their local area in the immediate future.

Research by Millennial Media, a mobile ad network that facilitates the planning and buying of mobile display campaigns, indicates that iOS and Android devices produce the best results when it comes to mobile advertising response rates. BlackBerry follows closely behind, with Windows rounding out the pack. These results are subject to change, of course, but for now, iOS, Android, BlackBerry, and Windows are reporting the best results from mobile display ads.[2]

Mobile Ad Network Providers

In the glory days of Madison Avenue during the twentieth century, if you wanted to run an ad campaign, the process was pretty simple: You'd call up the newspaper, a few radio stations, some TV networks, and perhaps a magazine or two, and pay to run the campaign. Given how streamlined the media planning and buying process was during those *Mad Men* days, it's no surprise the "mad men" had three martini lunches all the time; they had little else to do.

Today, media planning and buying is much more complex (and interesting). In order to be successful, you have to be intimately familiar with all the different ways it's now possible to distribute your ads. These channels might include dozens of radio networks, hundreds of cable channels, thousands of paid search campaigns, and millions of different websites. Perhaps the only way to deal with this complexity is to go back to drinking three martinis at lunch again. But, seriously, we think you get our point: Marketing in this century is so complex that it requires a statistician to keep track of everything.

To help with that, mobile ad networks were invented. A mobile ad network provides you, the marketer, with a network of "channels" (websites, apps, games, etc.) that attract the kinds of people you're interested in reaching—your target audience. For example, let's say you work at *Sports Illustrated* and want to reach men over the age of 25 who index high for their interest in sports. You'd contact a mobile ad network and have the professionals there plan and place the ad for you across hundreds, thousands, or even tens of thousands of websites, apps, and games.

There are dozens of mobile ad networks to choose from. Among the larger and more familiar are iAd from Apple, AdMob from Google, and Millennial Media, an independent. You'll also want to check out BuzzCity, CellTick, JumpTap, HipCricket, Medio, Mobclix, and Microsoft's ad network.

In addition, a few online publishers, such as the *Wall Street Journal*, CNN, the *New York Times*, and others sell mobile inventory on their own. This works great if you have a very simple mobile marketing program, or if you're buying one of these channels as a way to round out your offline marketing program. But if you really want to launch a successful mobile marketing campaign, you'll need to buy more than just a handful of publications; you'll also have to rely on a mobile advertising network.

Mobile Display Ad Specs

Mobile display ads come in all shapes and sizes. As of this writing, there are no one-size-fits-all standards, but the information in this section should give you a sense of the more common ones.

You can run standard display ads, which are just like the banner ads you see on traditional websites; or you can run rich media ads, which use video to enhance the experience. Also, with the advent of the iPad and other tablet computers, there are now two general categories of mobile display ads that you'll want to be familiar with: *smartphone display and rich media ads*, and *tablet display and rich media ads*. Here are the details on each:

Smartphone Display Ads
- *Large image banner:* 320 × 250 pixels. Images can be GIF, PNG, or JPEG, under 10KB file size. Animated GIF for animation.
- *Standard image banner:* 320 × 50 pixels; images can be GIF, PNG, or JPEG, under 10KB file size. Animated GIF for animation.
- *Medium image banner:* 168 × 42 pixels; images can be GIF, PNG, or JPEG, under 4KB file size. Animated GIF for animation.
- *Small image banner:* 120 × 30 pixels; images can be GIF, PNG, or JPEG, under 2KB file size. Animated GIF for animation.

◆ *Text tagline (optional):* Up to 24 characters for extra-large; up to 18 characters for large; up to 12 characters for medium; up to 10 characters for small. Not used for extra-extra-large.

Smartphone Rich Media Ads

◆ *Full-screen video:* 320 × 50/300 × 250 pixels; file size less than 3MB; maximum animation length: 30 seconds.

◆ *Slider video:* 320 × 50 pixels; file size less than 5KB (50 × 50) and less than 15KB (270 × 50); maximum animation length: 30 seconds.

◆ *Overlay:* 320 × 50 pixels that expand to 320 × 480 pixels; file size less than 20KB.

Tablet Display Ads

◆ *Extra-large horizontal image banner:* 728 × 90 pixels; images can be GIF, PNG, or JPEG, under 40KB file size. Animated GIF for animation.

◆ *Large square image banner:* 300 × 250 pixels; images can be GIF, PNG, or JPEG, under 40KB file size. Animated GIF for animation.

◆ *Skyscraper image banner:* 120 × 600 pixels; images can be GIF, PNG, or JPEG, under 40KB file size. Animated GIF for animation.

◆ *Medium horizontal image banner:* 468 × 60 pixels; images can be GIF, PNG, or JPEG, under 40KB file size. Animated GIF for animation.

◆ *Extra-large image banner:* 320 × 50 pixels; images can be GIF, PNG, or JPEG, under 10KB file size. Animated GIF for animation.

Tablet Rich Media Ads

◆ *In-line video:* 300 × 250 pixels; file size less than 40KB; maximum animation length: 30 seconds. User initiated on click.

◆ *Click-to-video:* 300 × 250/728 × 90/120 × 600/468 × 60; file size less than 3MB; maximum animation length: 30 seconds. User initiated on click.

◆ *Full-screen auto play:* 300 × 250/728 × 90/120 × 600/468 × 60; file size less than 3MB; maximum animation length: 30 seconds. Auto play.

Understanding the technical specs of a mobile display campaign is important, but what's really crucial is *what you do with the ads*. It's one thing to run a traditional mobile banner ad that's static; it's another thing entirely to run a banner ad that engages your prospects and converts them to customers.

Here are innovative techniques you can use to help drive more customers to your business:

◆ *Drive users to your location.* If you're interested in connecting prospects to brick-and-mortar locations, you're in luck. It's pretty easy to use GPS technology to identify where a prospect is located. Once the prospect clicks on your ad, he or she can be driven through to a map that identifies the store nearest to his or her current location. When the prospect clicks on the map, the contact information for that location is displayed on his or her smartphone. This technique is ideal for bookstores, car dealerships, auto repair shops, hardware stores, movie theaters. . . . Come to think of it, this technique is perfect for any brick-and-mortar business.

◆ *Connect users with your brand.* If you're looking for a way to get prospects and customers to interact with your brand, there's a simple technique you can use. Once they click your ad, they're taken to a screen that encourages them to upload a photo they've taken that shows them interacting with your product. You can then run promotions where, for example, the person who uploads a photo of him- or herself holding your product in the most exotic location wins a year's supply of your product. Variations on that theme are also fairly easy to execute.

◆ *Run a viral coupon promotion.* Interested in driving a lot of business to your location? Why not run a display ad that allows users to send an SMS text message to themselves and to their friends, complete with a discount code embedded in the message. Once people receive the code they can keep it on their phones until they arrive at your location. Best of all, they can forward it to friends who will also take advantage of the promotion. Remember to include an expiration date for the promotion so that it caps the length of the discount.

◆ *Become part of your prospect's contact list.* Wouldn't it be great if you could get your company contact information added to your prospects' contact lists on their phones? Bingo; consider it done. Simply run a display ad that sends a push notification to those people who clicked your ad asking for permission to add your contact information to their phones. From that point on, you're in their databases, giving them easy access to your contact information. This is perfect for B2C as well as B2B companies looking to open up a channel of easy communication with prospects and customers.

◆ *Run an e-mail promotion:* One of the best features of digital communications is that, in many cases, it costs virtually nothing to expand your reach. When users click on your ad, you can encourage them to spread the word about your promotion by e-mailing friends. Imagine the impact on your bottom line if you run a restaurant that wants to drive people to your Cinco De Mayo event; or maybe you have a music venue that wants to drive ticket sales for an upcoming concert. By encouraging people to e-mail their friends, you're driving extra business to your company without spending a dime more on marketing.

◆ *Add an event to your prospect's calendar:* What if you're running a special sale that extends a few weekends out? What if you want prospects to mark their calendars for an arts or music festival? What if you work for a TV network that wants to promote the season premiere of a hit show? Good news; you can run a display ad that sends prospects a push notification that can add your event to their calendars. Once they approve the notification, your date is added to their calendars, followed by a reminder that pops up a few days or a few hours before the event.

◆ *Incorporate user photos into an ad:* Want to deepen your relationship with prospects and customers? One of the best ways to do that is to incorporate a photo of them into your ads.

All you have to do is run a display ad that encourages them to take a photo of themselves (preferably, in which they're using your product), which they can then upload into a customized version of your ad. This is a great way to make your brand a bigger part of your prospects' and customers' lives.

Now that we've covered many of the cool ways you can use display ads to connect with prospects and customers, let's talk about another really interesting aspect of mobile display advertising: targeting.

Targeting Options for Mobile Display Ads

In doing research for this book, we interviewed Raphael Rivilla, the chief digital officer at BKV Digital and Direct Response. Raphael is an expert on all things mobile, particularly mobile media planning and buying. He says that there are so many options for targeting people with mobile media that it's often hard for marketing directors to figure out where to start.

Do you want to target people who visit only the top 100 websites? Sure, you can do that. What about targeting only AT&T customers? No problem. How about targeting only Android users? Yup, that's easy, too.

It gets even better. Do you want to target according to WiFi usage? For example, do you want to send an ad to business travelers who are accessing the Internet via mobile devices in airports across the globe? You can do that. What about wealthy individuals who are vacationing in high-end resorts? You can do that, too.

You can target by time of day; you can target people who have recently switched mobile service providers; you can even target people who are within a very narrowly defined geographic location (ideal for restaurants, bars, coffee shops, and other small, local businesses).

And still there's more. What if you were interested in targeting people who have exhibited certain behaviors? For example, let's say you wanted to target only those people who were reading an article on CNN's mobile site and who had previously clicked through on an ad for a red Chrysler convertible. You could do that; no problem.

Then we asked Raphael this: "What if we wanted to reach only doctors who owned Mercedes-Benz automobiles, who lived within five miles of the seashore, who make more than $250,000 a year, and who have downloaded the Food & Wine app to their iPads? Would that be possible?"

His answer was yes. He explained that by combining mobile targeting techniques with data available from companies like Experian and TransUnion, we could target those individuals precisely. He did, however, gloss over the fact that there are probably only 20 people in the United States who match those exact criteria, which would make a campaign defined that tightly impractical. But you get our point: You can target very specifically using mobile display ads. And the more tightly you define your campaign parameters, the more interest your prospects probably have in your product or service, which ultimately will improve the ROI of your campaign.

Buying Mobile Display Ads

You can buy mobile display ads in a variety of ways: CPM (cost-per-thousand impressions), CPC (cost-per-click) or CPA (cost-per-acquisition). Let's take a look at which type of mobile display ad might work best for your company.

◆ *CPM:* When you buy on a CPM basis, you're basically buying a guaranteed number of impressions. By "impression" we're referring to the number of times your ad is displayed to an individual. For example, if you're buying ads on CNN.com and paying a $3 CPM, then you're paying $3 for every 1,000 people who see your ad. (Before you run out to CNN with $3 in your hand, please remember that there are minimum "spends," and that you have to show your ad to tens of thousands, or hundreds of thousands, of people before the economics of a CPM approach work out.) Buying on a CPM basis is good if you're interested in creating brand awareness for your product or service. It's less effective if you're interested in driving people to a mobile site where they could buy something, like a book, a song, or an event ticket. For that, you'd probably want to use CPC or CPA.

◆ *CPC:* Buying on a cost-per-click basis is the way to go if want to pay Google, Yahoo!, or Bing *only* when someone clicks on your ad. In other words, you can run an ad on Google and agree to pay the company 25 cents for every person who clicks through on your ad. It might take 100 people to click through on your ad to make a sale, but if it costs you $25 (i.e., 25 cents × 100 clicks) to sell a product for $250, then it's a no-brainer—fire away. Interestingly, CPC is also a good idea if you're *not* expecting a lot of click-throughs on your ad. Why would you want to run a CPC ad that doesn't get a lot of click-throughs? Because you're still getting the brand imagery associated with your ad. In other words, tens of thousands of people are seeing your brand name on the ad, and assuming they don't click through, you don't pay a dime. It sounds crazy, but it's true.

◆ *CPA:* Cost-per-acquisition (also known as cost-per-engagement or cost-per-download) ensures that your mobile marketing campaign will deliver the exact action you're seeking: *You only pay when someone actually buys your product.* Now, before you jump out of your seat and run off to find a CPA deal, understand that there's more to it than meets the eye. Companies that will run CPA programs for you will often charge set-up costs, which run into the tens of thousands of dollars. Nothing is free. Well, except air. And love. But other than that, most things cost money.

Mobile Video

Mobile videos can run before, during, or after a visitor has clicked through to content on a mobile site. They can also be embedded within mobile display ads.

A terrific example in the effective use of mobile video is Pandora, the online radio station that plays music selections based on your individual taste. At various times during a user's engagement with Pandora, the station will run short video ads on the site. These short ads are great for enabling marketers to introduce their products to new customers. Better still, data can be tracked when a user clicks through on the video to your company website.

Animal Planet used mobile video to build awareness of its *River Monsters* series. The video was part of an integrated campaign that ran across multiple platforms, including a YouTube campaign that generated more than 900,000 views in the weeks leading up to the premiere. Animal Planet created interactive video ads on the AdMob network that gave viewers the opportunity to watch a preview of the *River Monsters* show, share the video through social media, learn more about the show's mobile website, and watch additional videos, all from within the mobile ad.

The Animal Planet campaign was a huge success. Mobile videos promoting the show generated more than 3 million impressions, with 84 percent of viewers watching the entire video. Interactive video ads on the AdMob network generated another 6 million impressions, with 75,000 users engaging with one of the interactive elements in the ad creative.[3]

If you're planning to use mobile video as part of your mobile marketing campaign, you'll want to make sure to keep a few best practices in mind. For starters, verify that your video will render well on a small screen. (For example, dark and fast-moving images won't appear clearly on a mobile device.) Also, keep video ads very short. Ten seconds is considered an eternity for a mobile video ad; 15 seconds is an eternity and beyond; 30 seconds . . . well, you get the idea. Keep 'em short.

One other factor to keep in mind is what the postclick experience will be like. Many businesses focus so much attention on the production of the video that they forget to put any emphasis on the postvideo experience. That's a no-no.

Mobile Display: The Most Important Part of Your Campaign

You might find it tempting to breeze through this chapter, but that would be a mistake. While mobile apps, mobile websites, and location-based services like foursquare are getting a lot of the positive press about mobile marketing, the heavy lifting is done in the mobile display world. Think of it this way: Fighter pilots may get all the attention, but no war was ever won without the support of the ground troops. Think of mobile display as your ground troops; it's the nuts-and-bolts side of the equation—but, man, those are some important nuts and bolts.

Do This:

♦ Visit the websites of the better-known ad networks and snoop around. There's plenty of helpful information on their sites. Then, call them up and engage with one of their salespeople. They'll offer additional advice and information.

♦ Be innovative with your approach to mobile display. People will eventually grow weary of display ads that simply link to a mobile webpage. Be more inventive; drive viewers to a free MP3 download, for example, or to a scavenger hunt or a discount coupon.

♦ Leverage some of the targeting opportunities that mobile display provides. The more your ad appeals to a certain segment, the more likely it will meet with success.

Don't Do This:

♦ Don't focus all your attention on mobile websites, mobile apps, and other "sexy" tools. Mobile display is an important component of most successful, well-rounded mobile marketing campaigns.

Notes

1. www.borrellassociates.com/reports/marketdata/smmobile-lar; accessed October 25, 2011.
2. www.millennialmedia.com/research; accessed October 25, 2011.
3. www.google.com/adwords/watchthisspace/creative-corner/case-studies/animal-planet; accessed October 25, 2011.

Chapter 13

How to Use Mobile Paid Search to Drive Customers to Your Business

Chances are, paid search will play an important role in your overall mobile marketing campaign. Why? Because one of the easiest ways to connect with mobile prospects and customers is through search. When people are in their cars or walking through a mall and need to locate a nearby retail store, they frequently grab their mobile devices and do a search.

Wouldn't you like your company to appear front and center when prospects are conducting mobile searches for the product or service you sell? (The answer to that would be yes.)

What makes mobile paid search even more appealing is that it's currently an underutilized tool. By that we mean it still hasn't reached a point of oversaturation, causing bids on keywords to go sky-high; there are still plenty of good deals still out there, meaning that you can still get keywords at a reasonable price. (More on buying keywords later in the chapter.)

But we're getting ahead of ourselves. Let's take a step back and examine paid search in general before we take a look at mobile paid search specifically.

Is Paid Search Right for You?

Paid search is traditionally a very good tool for companies that sell products online, that need to generate leads for their sales forces, or that have customers who research new products and services on Google, Bing, or Yahoo!

Let's take a look at a few specific examples. Paid search is ideal if yours is an e-commerce company that's selling items like cameras, shoes, clothing, books, and other similar tangibles. It's also good if your sales force sells insurance, cars, copiers, office supplies, or other comparable products. And it's good if your company's customers automatically go online when they need more information about a product or service from, for example, airlines, apartment complexes, and hospitality- and health-related companies.

But the focus shifts slightly when companies use *mobile* paid search to sell their products and services. When people use their mobile devices, they are looking for quick information on inexpensive or low-consideration products or services. They're intending to make immediate use of the information they find, whether it's about ordering pizza, dining out, or purchasing movie tickets. They're probably not planning to compare ratings and reviews on washing machines, or apply for a car loan.

It's also important to note that when they're using their mobile devices, people aren't inclined to do "long-tail" keyword searches. A long-tail keyword search is something like "best, midpriced spas and hotels catering to seniors in Paris." On a mobile device that search would be truncated to something like "spas in Paris for seniors" or even "Paris spas." Another important factor is that people doing searches on mobile devices are often doing so by voice, so keep in mind that someone doing a mobile voice search for "funny 60-second TV commercials" might end up getting "funny 62nd TV commercials."

What Is a Landing Page?

You've heard us talk about landing pages a good deal. A landing page is one that appears when a customer clicks on a banner (display) ad or a paid search ad. They're also known as *lead capture pages*.

> Landing pages are specifically set up to match the ad that was used to drive prospects to the page.
>
> A common mistake is to run a banner ad or paid search ad that drives prospects to a generic home page. That's a no-no and will result in less-than-optimal results.

Setting Up a Mobile Paid Search Campaign

Let's start with a recap of paid search fundamentals. Paid search is essentially an automated auction that gives you the opportunity to run ads and pay for those ads only when someone clicks on them. You write your ads and then choose relevant keywords to attract people to your ads. (A keyword is the search term or phrase that a person types or speaks into a search engine. The search engine matches their keyword search to ads or websites that are relevant to their request.)

On a desktop computer, the paid search ads appear above *and* to the right of the organic search results. On a mobile device, the paid search ads appear *only above* the organic search ads.

Google, Bing, and Yahoo! reward advertisers top positions based on their *bidding price* plus their *quality score*. The quality score is basically a way for search engines to determine whether your ad was relevant to users. More specifically, it's a complex formula that calculates how many people clicked on your ad and how involved they were with your site once they clicked through. If people click on your ad and then bounce off quickly, that's a sign to a search engine that the landing page wasn't very, or entirely, relevant to the user. As a result, the search engines will lower your quality score.

If a person stays on the landing page for an extended period of time, that's a sign it is relevant to the user, in which case search engines increase your quality score, recognition that the landing page has been helpful to the person who clicked the ad. When your quality score goes up, so does your search ranking on the page. That's good news for you and for your business, so it's important to make sure that your landing page delivers on the "promise" of your ad. In other words, if your ad says "Discounted Shoes" but the landing page doesn't mention discounted shoes, people will bounce off quickly; subsequently, your quality score will drop. But if the ad says

"Discounted Shoes" and the landing page is all about discounted shoes, people will stay on the page to explore different shoes, and your quality score will rise.

When you're setting up your mobile search program, it's important to structure your account properly. If you end up using mobile search frequently, some preplanning at this stage of the game will go a long way toward making your life simpler in the long run.

How should you set up your account? There are three levels in your account structure: the account level, the campaign level, and the ad group level. The *account level* is at the top and is simply a way of identifying the paid search account as being owned by a specific company or brand. In other words, if you run a printing business called Pro Graphics Communications, then your account level would be—you guessed it—Pro Graphics Communications. That said, if you're the brand manager for Crest Toothpaste at Procter & Gamble, your account level wouldn't be Procter & Gamble; it would be Crest Toothpaste, since that's the product or brand that "owns" the account.

Tips for Creating a Well-Structured Account Group

Here are some best practices for creating a winning account group:

◆ Always keep your account structure in mind: account level at the top, followed by campaigns, followed by ad groups.

◆ Give each campaign an easy-to-remember name that quickly identifies what it's for (e.g., "Spring Promotion").

◆ Split each campaign into ad groups that are subcategories of the campaign (e.g., "Spring Promotion" → "March Specials").

◆ Aim to have at least three ad groups per campaign. That way, each group will be more finely targeted and relevant to your prospect's needs (e.g., "Spring Promotion March Specials," "April Specials," "May Specials").

The next level down from the account level is the *campaign level*. This is where you'll break out your campaigns into categories that will help you stay organized in the future. Each campaign should focus on a specific area of your business or on a specific marketing campaign. For example, if you're a florist, you'll want to break out your campaigns based on certain groupings—for example, Valentine's Day Promotions, Wedding Promotions, New Year Promotions. By creating these campaign categories, you'll be able to keep things organized as you move forward.

Below the campaign level is the *ad group level*. These are the different ads you'll run in your paid search campaign. Staying with the florist example, underneath your Valentine's Day Promotions campaign, you might have three different ad groups: Roses, Tulips, and Daisies. To take the example further, you could create ad groups around the recipient's needs: For Spouses, For Girlfriends/ Boyfriends, For Family.

One thing you'll definitely want to do for a mobile paid search campaign is to create a separate campaign that targets only mobile devices. There are three benefits to doing so:

1. You'll be able to control ads that are shown to mobile users.
2. Your keyword bids will apply *only* to mobile searches.
3. It'll be easy to compare your mobile ad performance against other campaigns in your account.

Once you've got your account structure set up, you're ready to move on to the fun stuff: reaching the right customers—that is, your target audience. The primary way you'll be able to do that is by building a mobile-friendly keyword list.

Keywords: The Foundation of Your Campaign

Keywords are what grab the attention of potential customers and draw them into your ad. Despite what you may think, a small group of carefully targeted keywords will work better than a large group of untargeted keywords. For example, an ad group with the theme "Valentine's Day Roses" should only contain keywords specifically related to that topic, not to Valentine's Day in general.

How many keywords should you have in each group? There are no hard-and-fast rules, but Google indicates that aiming for between 5 and 50 keywords per ad group seems to work best. And, remember, mobile search is different from desktop search; the mobile keypad is small, and people using mobile devices are in a hurry and tend to act on the information they get right away, so keep your keywords short. Think about using Google's Keyword Tool to drill down and gain insights on terms people use on mobile devices.

Mobile Search Is Different from Regular Search

Google's Keyword Tool lets you research the keywords people use frequently on their mobile devices, versus their desktops or laptops.

When developing keywords for your mobile paid search campaign, remember that people are often searching for information they want to use immediately.

With that in mind, be sure to add the following to your keyword lists: "locations" (e.g., "Pizza Hut locations"), addresses (e.g., "Walmart on Peachtree Street"), zip codes, and urgency terms (e.g., "plumbing emergency repair").

When choosing your keywords, you can match them up using either *broad match* or *negative match*. These options give you greater control over when your ads will appear.

Broad match reaches the most users by displaying your ad whenever your keyword or a variation of your keyword is searched. For instance, if your keyword phrase is "Valentine's Day Roses," it will trigger your ad on searches for "roses for Valentine's Day," "red roses Valentine's Day," or "send roses for Valentine's Day."

Negative match *prevents* your ad from appearing for a specific keyword. For instance, if you specify "synthetic" as a negative keyword match, then your ad won't display when someone searches for "synthetic roses for Valentine's Day." (An aside: If you ever find yourself shopping for synthetic roses for Valentine's Day, save yourself the trouble. The person you're buying them for will *not* appreciate your synthetic gift. Trust us—we learned this the hard way.)

Creating a Mobile Keyword List

When you're creating a keyword list for your mobile campaign, it's a good idea to consider what people might be doing when they're searching from their mobile devices. We've said previously that they're "on the go," but we can take that a step further. For instance, they probably want information quickly and plan to act upon it right away. They're not looking for long, in-depth answers to questions about your corporate philosophy, for example. What they *are* looking for are short, quick answers about, say, your street address, your phone number, or your customer service department.

Let's take a look at how to go about buying mobile keywords from Google, Bing, or Yahoo!:

1. *List all the relevant keywords for your campaign.* Again, staying with the florist example, you'd want to list all the keywords and keyword phrases that might attract people doing searches for florists. This would include such obvious terms as "florist" and "flowers for birthday," but it would also include broader terms like "anniversary gifts" and "birthday gift ideas."

2. *Split your keywords into themed ad groups.* Florists typically have seasons when their sales skyrocket (e.g., Valentine's Day) but they also have nonseasonal triggers, too. In keeping with this example, you'd want to divide your keyword ad groups by themes. Of course, one theme would be Valentine's Day; other themes might include Birthday Gifts, Special Offers, and Summer Promotions.

3. *Refine your list.* Once you've completed the first two steps, it's time to review and refine your list. For example, you won't want to bid on terms like "flowers," because your ad would show up every time a gardener, horticulture student, or floral

painter did a search on that term. You'll also want to avoid using the same keyword in multiple ad groups within the same campaign, as that would effectively put you in competition with yourself. (Why is that a bad thing? Because you'd artificially bid up the price on the keyword.) Also, using negative-match keywords like "free" will prevent your ad from appearing when someone is looking for free stuff. People looking for free stuff are not in your target market. You're trying to make some money, right?

Click-Through Rate versus Conversion Rate

Your click-through rate (CTR) is an indication of how many people actually clicked on your ad. CTR is calculated by taking the number of clicks and dividing it by the number of impressions (the number of people who saw the ad in the first place).

Your conversion rate (CR) is an indication of the number of people who clicked on the ad and then purchased your product. CR is calculated by taking the number of purchases and dividing it by the total number of people who clicked on the ad and visited the landing page.

Writing Ads—The Fun Stuff

You will drive traffic to your mobile site based, in part, on the ads you write for your mobile paid search campaign. Thus, the better the ad, the more traffic you'll generate. Clearly, then, it's a good idea to put some serious thought into the ads you write.

One of the terrific aspects of mobile paid search (or any paid search, for that matter), is that you can A/B split test your ads. What's an A/B split test? It's the process of creating two versions of the same ad and making a minor change in one of them. For instance, you could write an ad with a headline that reads, "Valentine's Day Special," and another one with the same body copy but with a headline that reads, "Valentine's Day Flowers." By making this minor change, you'll get a sense of which ad performed better.

By testing the ads this way you'll be able to determine which one drove the most click-throughs and conversions. You might assume that the ad with "Special" in the headline would come out ahead because it telegraphs the message that there's a discount; but you never know. Every time you think you've got marketing all figured out, some new twist comes along to keep you humble.

Tips on Setting Up Your Mobile Campaign

Be sure to separate your regular desktop search campaign from your mobile search campaign. That way, you can track your results and improve efficiencies.

Also, you can target your ads by carrier, so be sure to test various carriers to see if the users behave differently with each of them.

The best approach to testing ads is to write three or four variations of the same ad (essentially doing an A/B/C/D split test). And make sure to run the ads with the same set of keywords, because your purpose is to test the *ads* not the *keywords*. Also be aware that if you have more than one ad in each of your ad groups, Google and other search engines will rotate them for you at no additional cost.

Be sure to allow your ad variations to run for a while before analyzing your clicks. How long is a "while"? A good rule of thumb is five to seven days before you conduct any deep analysis. Ultimately, the ads that have the highest click-through rate will give you an indication of which of them "pulled" the best. That said, it's not just the CTR you're interested in; you're also trying to determine which ad *converted* the best—that is, converted prospects to sales.

If you intend to measure your click-through and conversion rates, be sure to test for only one variable. In other words, take care to swap out only the headline, or the offer, or the call to action. And, remember, for our purposes here, you're going to keep the landing page exactly the same; you're doing a split test on the ads, not the landing pages. (When you're ready to do a split test on landing pages, you can create two landing pages and test which of those performs the best.)

TIPS ON WRITING ADS

As you become more knowledgeable about using mobile paid search to drive customers to your business, you'll get a sense of what works and what doesn't. The results of your ad-writing efforts will be, literally, staring you in the face each day when you check your numbers. To improve the chances that you like what you see, follow these tips, as they can give you a head start on what works and what doesn't in the mobile paid search arena.

◆ *Write headlines that focus on your product, not your company.* A common mistake many people make when writing their first paid search ad is to focus on their *company* instead of the *product* or *service* they're promoting. Remember, people aren't buying your company; they're buying your product or service. And, preferably, they're buying what you're selling at some sort of discount. So be sure to focus the ad on your product or your special, not on your company. Good: *Valentine's Day Specials.* Not So Good: *Peachtree Road Florist.*

◆ *Describe benefits in the body copy.* Your ad should help people understand why your product or service is exactly what they're looking for. Focus on the specific *benefits* they'll gain by buying your product or service; don't use generic, too-general terms. Good: *Same-day delivery.* Not So Good: *Beautiful roses.*

◆ *Always include a call to action.* Research shows that ads perform better when a specific CTA is featured prominently in the copy. And in your call to action, be sure to impose a sense of urgency; for example, you'll get better results when you give people a deadline. Good: *Click now for discount.* Not So Good: *In business 25 years.* (Who cares? Customers want to know what you can do for them *today.*)

◆ *Make sure the ad links to a landing page, not your home page.* To continue with the florist example, the objective would be to ensure that the person who clicked on your ad landed on a page that was selling Valentine's Day flowers at a discount.

Driving people through to a generic home page is a waste of money. Good: *A promotion-specific URL*. No So Good: *A generic home page URL*.

♦ *Include keywords in your ad.* According to Google, the best-performing ads are those in which keywords are used in the headlines. For instance, if you're running an ad that has "Valentine's Day discounts" as a keyword phrase, you'll want to also feature that phrase in the headline of your paid search ad. That way, the consumer knows the ad specifically matches what he or she searched for. Good: *Using keywords in your headline*. Not So Good: *Not using keywords in your headlines*.

Measuring the Success of Your Campaign

One of the great advantageous of mobile marketing is that it's digital, for digital is easy to track. In fact, the very first thing you should do when you're setting up a mobile paid search campaign is to figure out how you're going to track the results of your campaign.

With that in mind, here are important statistics you should be measuring from your paid search campaign:

♦ *Click-through rate (CTR):* As mentioned earlier, your CTR is one of the fundamental numbers you should be keeping an eye on. As a rule of thumb, a CTR of less than 1 percent means your ad is not targeted properly. In other words, the ad you've written isn't matching the keywords people are searching for. If you have a CTR of below 1 percent, then you'll want to double-check that the keywords (e.g., "Valentine's Day specials") match what your ads are promoting (e.g., "Valentine's Day sale").

♦ *Average position:* Be sure to check your average position to find out where you ad is appearing on the search results page. On a regular paid search campaign, up to 11 ads are shown on any given page; on mobile devices, only 2 or 3 appear. If your average position in your mobile paid search campaign isn't better than 3, you're ad is not really showing up where it should be.

♦ *Quality score:* Google uses a quality score to calculate how relevant your ad is to searchers. The higher your quality score, the higher position your ad will rank, and the lower your costs. You can ensure a high-quality score by making your ads entirely relevant to the consumer. The more relevant they are, the more clicks, and the higher your quality score.

◆ *Conversion tracking:* Ideally, all roads in mobile paid search should lead to conversions. A conversion, in the classical sense, is when a customer buys your product. For mobile paid search purposes, you may have to provide a coupon to track conversions. In other words, because many mobile users are searching for locations (rather than e-commerce web pages), you can't really sell to them via your mobile landing page. What's a business to do? Simply, provide a mobile coupon on the landing page that can be scanned (and, thus, tracked) at your store's location. This enables you both to drive people to your location and measure the results of your campaign when the coupon is scanned. (If yours is a B2B company, you can still track results by providing a click-to-call phone number or by creating a *very simple* form on which people can ask for a sales representative to call them back.)

As we said at the beginning of the chapter, mobile paid search is currently an underutilized tool, as marketers continue to focus a great deal of attention on mobile websites and mobile apps. The result is that mobile paid search doesn't get the respect it deserves. That's to your advantage; as long as mobile paid search flies under the radar, there are still plenty of inexpensive keywords available for you to use to drive customers to your mobile landing pages.

What are you waiting for? Give Google, Bing, or Yahoo! a try!

Do This:

◆ Set up your account properly. When builders construct a house, they spend a good deal of time laying the foundation. Why? Because they know a solid foundation is critical for a sturdy home. Your account structure is like the foundation on a house; a little extra effort here goes a long way.

◆ Track your results. There's no point running a mobile paid search campaign if you're not going to track the results. Be sure to monitor your click-through rate, as well as your conversion rate. By doing so, you'll be able to accurately calculate your ROI.

◆ Include a call to action. All good paid search ads have a strong CTA. Be sure to use active phrases like "Buy Online Now" and "Order Yours Today."

Don't Do This:

◆ Don't pay good money for generic keywords. If you're a florist promoting roses for Valentine's Day, keywords such as "roses" will attract everyone from gardeners to Guns N' Roses enthusiasts. Be more specific: "Valentine's Day roses" or "anniversary roses" will work much more effectively.

Chapter 14

Location-Based Marketing

LBS, NFC, Bluetooth, and LBA—Oh My!

W ouldn't it be great if you could send a special discount to individuals when they walked past your store? Wouldn't it be terrific if you could send a client a special greeting when he or she entered your office lobby? And wouldn't it be awesome if you could reward your most loyal customers with instant mobile coupons?

Good news. All that, and more, is possible with *location-based marketing*, which includes location-based services, near field communications, Bluetooth marketing, and location-based advertising.

Location-based marketing is positioned to have a huge impact on how marketers reach out to consumers, thanks to its capability to customize marketing messages based on a prospect's location and preferences (see Figure 14.1).

With that in mind, let's take a quick look at each of the tools just mentioned.

Location-Based Marketing Tools

LOCATION-BASED SERVICES (LBS)

These are typically mobile apps that provide information or entertainment to users based on their location. Some of the best-known LBS apps include foursquare, FriendsAround, and SCVNGR, which

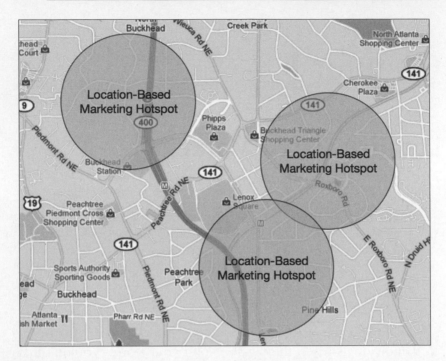

Figure 14.1 Location-based marketing allows you to market to customers based on their proximity to certain hotspots. It's ideal for brick-and-mortar locations interested in driving foot traffic to their stores.

allow users to check in at a location and, as a result, qualify for coupons or discounts. Other LBS apps include Localmind, which allows users to find out what's happening at bars, restaurants, and other retail locations in their neighborhoods; and Ditto!, which enables users to exchange recommendations about movies, restaurants, and other venues.

One of the best-known examples of a successful LBS promotion was Chili's use of foursquare to send coupons for free cheese dip to anyone who checked in at the restaurant chain's locations. Recall from Chapter 1, where we first described this promotion, that Chili's took it a step further and provided the same coupon to anyone who checked in at another eatery within 200 yards of one of its restaurants. The result was that the chain was able to make a special offer to potential customers who were right around the corner from any of its locations.

NEAR FIELD COMMUNICATIONS (NFC)

Interested in exchanging contact information quickly from your mobile device to another person's mobile device? Would you like to share family photos wirelessly with a friend? NFC allows you to do that.

The NFC technology lets two devices that are within close proximity (between 2 and 20 centimeters away) exchange information. If you have Google+ loaded onto certain smartphones, you can exchange contact information with other users simply by placing the phones next to each other. In addition, with an NFC-enabled device you can make payments using Google Wallet or PayPal. Just tap your phone into the NFC transmitter at the retail location and, after you've entered your security information, you can pay for your items.

BLUETOOTH MARKETING

This technology, like NFC, allows data transfer over short distances. If you've ever used a wireless phone headset, you were probably using Bluetooth. Or if you've ever exchanged contact information using the mobile app called Bump, probably you were using Bluetooth, too.

Bluetooth is different from NFC in that it can communicate over longer distances. Where, as noted, NFC can communicate with other devices between 2 and 20 centimeters away, Bluetooth can extend up to 10 meters away. In addition, Bluetooth can exchange more information per second than NFC.

In a nutshell, NFC is terrific for exchanging quick, short bursts of information; Bluetooth is better for more robust bursts of information over longer distances.

LOCATION-BASED ADVERTISING (LBA)

LBA isn't a technology as much as it's a form of advertising. What do we mean by that? LBA uses various tools, such as GPS and geo-fencing, to locate people who might be prospects and send them messages.

For instance, say you're in charge of marketing for a clothing store chain and you want to run a mobile display ad that targets prospects when they're within walking distance of your location. You can do that using LBA. All you'd have to do is provide your mobile ad network provider with a list of your store locations. By using geo-fencing, the ad network knows when someone is within proximity of one of your stores. The result is that the prospective customers who are surfing the Net on their mobile devices will see a banner ad letting them know that your clothing store is half a mile away and is running a 25 percent off special on athletic socks.

Sorting through the Location-Based Marketing Maze

It's easy to get a little confused when you're learning about location-based marketing. Just to get started, you have to be familiar with LBS, NFC, Bluetooth, and LBA—and we haven't even mentioned related tools like WiFi or RFID.

To ease your confusion and, at the same time, give you a little background on when and how you're most likely to use each of these tools, read through the following descriptions.

♦ *Location-based services (LBS):* If your business wants to drive customers to your brick-and-mortar location, or if you want to provide discounts to customers who frequent your stores, then you'll want to take a deeper dive into LBS. These tools have been adopted by a younger, mobile-savvy crowd, so they're especially effective if your target market skews toward the 18- to 34-year-old crowd.

♦ *Near field communications (NFC):* If your business is interested in providing mobile payment options to your customers, or if you're looking for an alternative to a semiclunky QR code campaign, then you'll want to look into NFC. Mobile payments using NFC are being adopted by consumers as we speak. And, in the near future, in-store posters, subway billboards, and even tombstones will include NFC chips that transmit information to people who wave their phones near the chips.

♦ *Bluetooth marketing:* If you're someone who wants or needs to exchange contact information, music files, or photographs with other people, or if your business wants to make it easy to transmit information to its clients wirelessly, then you'll want to explore Bluetooth technology. Bluetooth is capable of transmitting large amounts of information over longer distances than NFC, so it's great for a wide variety of businesses.

It's especially useful if you're in the B2B world and would like to transfer large documents or files to your clients.

◆ *Location-based advertising (LBA):* If getting involved in LBS, NFC, and Bluetooth seems too complex and time-consuming for you right now, no worries. LBA is a perfectly good alternative, and best of all, it's easy to execute. LBA is ideal for companies that want to attract prospects who are in their immediate vicinity—for example, car dealerships, real estate agents, insurance agents, or a brick-and-mortar retailers. Just contact your mobile ad network provider and they'll walk you through the details of executing a campaign.

How Companies Are Using Location-Based Marketing to Connect with Customers

There are a lot of different ways companies are using location-based marketing to connect with customers. Some tend to stick with only one of the tools, to keep things simple. Others utilize all of the tools as a way to stay connected with their customers on a variety of fronts.

The best way to explain the various approaches companies are taking with location-based marketing is to share case studies of a number of them that have successfully used location-based marketing to grow their sales and revenue.

USING LBA TO IMPROVE CUSTOMER LOYALTY

In the United Kingdom, the restaurant chain Subway launched a location-based marketing campaign called "You Are Here." The campaign used LBA and MMS to targeted users who were within close proximity of a Subway restaurant. Users had to opt in first (always an important consideration for a location-based marketing campaign), and once they had done so were sent MMS messages to alert them to special discounts when they were walking by a Subway location.

In a sense, Subway went to its existing customers and said, "Hey, next time you're near one of our restaurants, do you want us to send you a text with a special discount on it?" By confirming they were interested in receiving the messages, customers were, essentially, giving Subway permission to send them discounts whenever they were within walking distance of a location.

Using LBS to Generate Public Relations Buzz

Designer shoemaker Jimmy Choo teamed up with foursquare to create a scavenger hunt in London. Contestants went online to follow the foursquare check-ins being conducted by Jimmy Choo employees. If contestants were able to get to the stores before the employees left, they won a pair of shoes in the size and style of their choice.

Winners simply had to approach Jimmy Choo representatives and say, "I've been following you." By using that "secret" password phrase, the pair of shoes was theirs.

Using NFC Communications to Improve Customer Experience and Secure Brand Loyalty

Zuma Fashions rolled out an NFC campaign that embedded chips into point-of-sale posters. Consumers were encouraged to download the Zuma Fashions app from iTunes or the Android Marketplace. Once loaded, customers "swiped" their handsets over the NFC chip and were encouraged to fill out a short survey. After they'd filled out the survey, they were given a digital discount that they could use right away.

The campaign proved so successful that Zuma extended it; customers could, for example, swipe NFC tags attached to blouses and get details on the price of the garment and the materials used in its construction, and watch a short video of it being modeled. Ultimately, the app made it possible for Zuma to create a loyalty program for people who frequented stores.

Using an LBS App to Improve Customer Loyalty and Drive Repeat Sales

When most people think of a location-based services app, the two that tend to come to mind are foursquare and SCVNGR. But pizza chain Domino's created its own app to drive sales for specific locations. First described in Chapter 2, it bears more detailed mention here.

How does the Domino's app work? First, let's do some math to determine how many pizza combinations the Domino's app would have to calculate. With 4 different pizza sizes, 4 different sauces, 22 different toppings, and numerous other add-ons, we calculated that there are *522 billion possible combinations*. (Seriously: 522 billion. It took us all night to count them.)

With that many different combinations, you can imagine the complexity of creating an app capable of handling the workload. But Domino's did it, streamlining the ordering process and making it as simple as possible. From a customer loyalty standpoint, the app is pure genius. Once customers take the time to download the app, input their information, and order a pizza, what's the likelihood they're going to start all over with a competitor's app? Very low.

The Domino's app proves an important point: Location-based marketing doesn't have to involve just *marketing;* sometimes it can involve a *transaction*, which in the long run will serve to reduce churn and improve customer loyalty.

Using LBS to Improve Brand Loyalty and Encourage Repeat Visits

LBS provider SCVNGR has introduced a program called LevelUp that encourages customers to come back for repeat visits. Southwest Day Spa in Boston decided to use the program to encourage its customers to come back again and again.

Here's how it works: Every time a customer comes in to Southwest Day Spa for a visit, she uses SCVNGR's LevelUp app to pay for the visit. (Customers preload funds onto the LevelUp app prior to using it to purchase products.) When they pay with LevelUp the first time, they get $5 applied to their second visit. The idea is that each time a customer comes back, she gets a larger discount, thus encouraging brand loyalty and repeat visits. So, for example, customers get $5 off their first visit, $10 off their second, and $15 off their third.

When you calculate the value of repeat visits from customers, the increase in discounts pays for itself.

Using Bluetooth Marketing to Generate Buzz and Brand Loyalty

Lynx, a U.K.-based maker of body sprays, is famous for its innovative marketing campaigns. To promote the launch of a new pocket-sized spray, the company's advertising agency installed highly visible floor vinyls in high-traffic areas of various colleges and universities. Students who stood on or near the Lynx floor vinyls were encouraged to wirelessly download a simple branded dating application via Bluetooth.

The campaign was a big success for the brand, not only because of the PR buzz it generated, but also because more than 500 students a day downloaded the app during the course of the campaign.

USING LBA TO STRENGTHEN LOYALTY AND DRIVE REVENUE

Outdoor clothing and gear supplier REI used ShopAlerts to engage consumers with time- and location-targeted messages. When consumers who had previously opted in to receive messages were near an REI location, they received SMS messages with special discounts at the store. A survey of ShopAlerts customers found that 69 percent of respondents said ShopAlerts would increase their likelihood to visit a store. What's more, 65 percent said they made a purchase because of ShopAlerts, and 73 percent said they would definitely or probably use the service in the future.[1]

Location-Based Marketing Best Practices

There are several best practices to consider as you set up your location-based marketing campaign. Some of them revolve around marketing fundamentals; others are more specific to this new and emerging field.

- *Address consumer confusion.* Most consumers will have a natural tendency to shy away from LBS, NFC, Bluetooth, and LBA campaigns. It's human nature to resist something you don't entirely understand. It's your job to explain the nature of the campaign and ensure them that it's safe and nonthreatening.
- *Provide clear opt-in instructions.* You may live and work in a world where mobile marketing is common, but most people don't. As such, you'll need to explain as quickly and clearly as possible to your prospects and customers how to opt in to your location-based marketing program. Spend extra effort ensuring prospects that they can opt out at any time.
- *Explain what to expect.* People don't mind getting marketing messages when they've opted in to receive. But they do mind being overwhelmed by too many messages and/or confusing offers. Explain to consumers what they can expect after they've

opted in to your program. That way, you'll avoid unpleasant surprises for your target audience.

♦ *Test the campaign on unbiased candidates:* Of course, you'll want to test your campaign yourself. But the most effective way to test it is give it a whirl with someone who doesn't know what to expect. This does not mean your spouse; he or she will be predisposed to approve of the program. The point is to test it on an objective subject—or 2 or 50. Testing your way to success is a good approach for any business.

♦ *Make it worth their while:* You're asking customers to opt in to your location-based marketing program, so reward them for their trouble. There's nothing more frustrating than opting in to a program only to find a better discount on a print ad or a direct mail postcard. If people go to the trouble to be part of your program, reward their loyalty with special discounts.

Right now, talk about mobile apps, mobile websites, and 2D codes dominate in the marketing landscape, but as time goes on, location-based marketing will eclipse these tools. Why? Because location-based marketing makes it possible to customize the user experience with a brand, and sophisticated companies understand that doing so strengthens loyalty and encourages purchases.

Once consumers get comfortable with LBS, NFC, Bluetooth, and LBA, the floodgates will open. In the future it will be commonplace to have an ad pop up on their mobile devices saying, for example, "Dave, we're glad you're back at McDonald's again this week. Would you like a special discount on the Caesar Salad Wrap you had on your last visit? Or would you like a 10 percent discount on a Banana Smoothie instead?"

Those days are not far away. And that prospect is very exciting indeed.

Do This:
♦ Call your ad agency or your mobile ad network provider; this is the easiest way to get started in location-based marketing. Explain that you'd like to launch a location-based advertising campaign. They'll walk you through the process.

◆ Approach a location-based services provider like foursquare and SCVNGR to run a promotion with them; this is the next-easiest step to take. They'll hold your hand to a certain degree, making the promotion easy to execute.

◆ Once you've run your LBA and LBS campaigns, get ready to dive into the world of NFC and Bluetooth. NFC chips can be embedded into point-of-sale promotions, and Bluetooth transmitters can be used in campaigns where data-transfer distances exceed 20 centimeters.

Don't Do This:

◆ Don't shy away from location-based marketing. It really *is* the future of mobile. It may be a while before it's widely adopted by consumers, but eventually they'll catch up and you want to be there to meet them.

◆ Always provide a mechanism for consumers to opt in before sending them messages. Mobile devices are very private items and people don't take kindly to companies that take advantage of their use.

Note

1. www.mobilemarketer.com/cms/news/research/7262.html; accessed October 25, 2011.

Chapter 15

Mobile Apps

A Great Way to Keep Them Coming Back for More

One of the first questions people ask when they decide to launch a mobile marketing campaign is, "Do I need my own app?"

The short answer is no, you don't have to have an app to get into mobile marketing. In fact, most businesses choose *not* to have an app, because they're labor-intensive and can be a challenge to produce.

That said, there are some surprisingly easy ways to become involved in app development. Before you begin, though, remember that there are already hundreds of thousands of apps available to iPhone, Android, BlackBerry, and Windows phone users, so if you're going to invest in an app for your business, be sure to reserve a good chunk of change to promote the app to prospective users.

What's the Difference Between a Mobile Website and an App?

We're glad you asked about the difference between a mobile website and an app because it's a question on a lot of people's minds these days. The short answer is that a mobile website is just like a regular website but designed for smaller screens. An app is a software program that's installed on a mobile device.

157

Now let's drill down on this distinction a little further. There are a few different ways to approach mobile websites. The first is to simply create a mobilized version of your regular website. This might include an About Us page, a Contact Us page, your blog, and a few other odds and ends.

The second approach to mobile website development is to create a site that has some additional functionality. For example, if you're a restaurant owner, you may want to create a mobile website that's entirely geared toward ordering takeout. In this case, there would be no need for an About Us page or a blog; just a way for people to scan your menu, click on their orders, and hit submit.

An app, on the other hand, is a program that's installed on your mobile device, much the same way you might install Garage Band or Microsoft Office on your desktop or laptop computer. An app needs to be created individually for each platform. In other words, if you want your app to run on the iOS, Android, BlackBerry, and Windows phone platforms, you'd have to create four different apps.

Another challenge with apps is that they must be submitted for approval by Apple, Google, RIM, and Microsoft. In many cases, this isn't too much of a hassle; but in some cases, it can be a real pain in the Apple. What's more, in order for users to use your app, they have to download it from the app store, which is just one more barrier to entry. Finally, every time you want to make changes to or upgrade your app, you have to go through an approval process again, which, though simplified, can still be challenging.

What Kind of App Is Right for You?

There are a variety mobile app types and each has its strengths and weaknesses. Here's a partial list of the kinds of mobile apps currently available on the marketplace:

- *Business utilities:* Business card scanners, calculators, spreadsheet programs, PDF readers, voice recording utilities, expense tracking, time tracking, and others
- *Financial tools:* Stock market apps, utility trading apps, currency converters, news providers, and others
- *Educational:* Maps, books, flash cards, calculators, dictionaries, and others

- *News and information:* TV and print newsfeeds, celebrity gossip, game highlights, stock information, and others
- *Weather:* Weather maps, forecasts, alerts, allergy reports, ozone reports, and others
- *Navigation and travel:* Traffic maps, flight information, currency exchange, alternate route finders, and others
- *Shopping:* Amazon, eBay, Scoutmob, movie tickets, bookstores, and others
- *Fun and games:* The Onion News Network, *People* magazine, Fandango, Monopoly, Spin the Coke, and *America's Got Talent*, to name a few
- *Social networking:* Facebook, LinkedIn, Twitter, and all the other usual suspects, plus applications that allow you to transfer information simply by bumping two smartphones together

Figure 15.1 shows a breakdown of use according to the various categories.

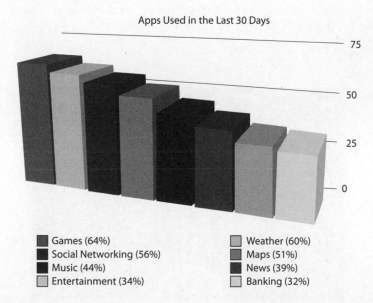

FIGURE 15.1 The most popular categories for apps are games, weather, social networking, maps, music, news, entertainment, and banking.

Source: Created by Jamie Turner. Research from Nielsen, "The State of Mobile Apps," http://blog.nielsen.com/nielsenwire/online_mobile/the-state-of-mobile-apps, June 1, 2010

How Coca-Cola Is Using Mobile Apps to Connect with Customers

The Coca-Cola Company introduced the PUSH! + Play app as part of its ongoing efforts to go mobile. The app is pretty simple to use: Customers are shown a series of bottle caps from various soft drinks provided by the Coca-Cola Company, including Fanta, Pibb, Sprite, and, of course, Coca-Cola.

People using the app are encouraged to memorize the order in which the bottle caps light up and beep (see Figure 15.2). After each go-round, a new beeping bottle cap is added. Players race against the clock to see how many bottle caps they can remember before time runs out.

The game is an effective one because it's easy to play and is habit-forming. (For any app to be successful, it has to be habit-forming; or, at a minimum, it has to give people a reason to use it over and over again.) The game also has a viral aspect to it, which helps keep it in front of new players. But what makes the app particularly useful for Coca-Cola from a marketing perspective is that it deepens the customer relationship with the brand by providing interesting trivia about Coca-Cola products between each session. Every time players hit the reset button, they're greeted by Coca-Cola trivia, such as the following.

FIGURE 15.2   The Coca-Cola Company uses apps like PUSH! + Play to connect with consumers and promote its brand image around the globe.

Coca-Cola first became an Olympic sponsor at the 1928 Amsterdam games.

We'll drink to this: The first time Coca-Cola was sold in bottles was 1894.

Fanta was first introduced in Italy before coming to the U.S.

The result is a double-whammy: The app provides a way for Coca-Cola to drive home its *happiness* positioning and provides the user memorable information about the Coca-Cola legacy.

This is not the first and only Coca-Cola app. In fact, it's one of more than three dozen different apps designed for the Coca-Cola Company's various brands. It's clear that the folks at Coke's Atlanta headquarters have decided that mobile apps are a terrific way to stay connected with their customers around the globe.

Generating Revenue with Appvertising

It's one thing to create apps that build brand awareness; it's another thing entirely to create an app that *generates revenue*. That's exactly what *AutoWeek* magazine did with its iPhone app.

How to Tell Whether an App Is Right for Your Business

Is your business right for app development? Yes, if:

◆ It's a large brand looking for ways to deepen its relationship with customers (e.g., Coca-Cola, Campbell's).
◆ It's a content provider looking for new distribution channels (e.g., *AutoWeek*, CNN).
◆ It has a game concept with the potential to go viral (e.g., Angry Birds, ABC Go).
◆ It has a utility that helps people execute tasks from their mobile devices (e.g., Charles Schwab, Dragon Dictation).
◆ The "business" is a celebrity interested in leveraging his or her brand (e.g., Jamie Oliver, Martha Stewart).

(continued)

(*continued*)

♦ It's a B2B company looking for new ways to connect with customers (e.g., UPS, FedEx).

♦ It's a B2C company seeking new revenue streams (e.g., Netflix, *New York Times*).

AutoWeek is a traditional magazine publisher that realized it needed to engage its readers on their mobile devices. The challenge was that mobile device users are often reluctant to pay for content delivered via mobile website or mobile app. To overcome this obstacle, *AutoWeek* partnered with AdMob (Google's advertising network) and created an app that would be monetized using mobile ads. *AutoWeek*'s goal was simply to recoup its app development costs by earning revenue from the ads placed on its app.

In order to hit the ground running, *AutoWeek* ran display ads that linked users directly to landing pages within the app store. *AutoWeek* also ran ads inside more than 3,000 apps available in AdMob's iPhone network. (Note: The new word for running ads inside mobile apps is *appvertising*.) Here, the goal was to drive the maximum number of downloads in as short a period of time as possible so the magazine could boost the app's ranking inside the app store.

What were the results? *AutoWeek* was able to recoup its app development costs and earn revenue within the first two months, thanks to its appvertising program. The campaign to boost the app's rankings within the app store also worked; in the United Kingdom, the app jumped from number 18 to number 5, and in Australia it jumped from number 90 to number 2.

All that said, it's important to realize that the odds of getting rich running ads inside apps is very, very slim. Remember, the twofold goal for *AutoWeek* was to: (1) recoup its initial investment so that it could (2) cost-effectively engage with readers on a new and emerging platform. In that sense, the campaign was a big success.

If you decide to invest in an app, your goal should be to *deepen your relationship with customers*, not become an instant millionaire. That's not to say that it's impossible to get rich from a hugely popular app. In fact, it does happen—every so often. But when you consider that for every app that makes someone rich there are tens of thousands of apps that generate zero revenue, you'll understand that the important idea behind apps isn't about getting rich; it's about providing new ways to connect with customers, with the ultimate purpose to deepen their relationship with your brand.

How to Build Your Own App

If you decide there's good reason to develop your own app, you need to know there are several ways to do it. The first step is to figure out which platform you'd like to use. Table 15.1 will help you get a sense of the key players in the app world.

Before you dive into the deep end of the app development pool, we recommend you familiarize yourself with a number of the more advanced mobile developer tools. Here's some background information on each platform.

Android OS developers: You can create apps using Java for Android by downloading its free software development kit. The kit comes with samples, source code, developer tools, and emulators for testing your app. Android even provides how-to videos, technical articles, and instructions on how to develop apps, just in case you're feeling a bit overwhelmed by it all. And, note, you'll have to pay a one-time $25 developer registration fee to distribute apps in the Android Marketplace.

Apple iOS: If you want to create an iPhone app using the iOS platform, you'll need to shell out about $99, which isn't much considering the elegance and functionality of the program. The iOS Developer Center has a wide selection of tools, tips,

TABLE 15.1   Key App Platforms

	Android	iOS	BlackBerry	Windows
Launched	November 2008	July 2008	April 2009	November 2009
Device Market Share	39%	28%	20%	9%
Number of Apps	250,000	500,000	25,000	18,000

Source: GetElastic.com, ReadWriteWeb.com, CNet.com, Nielsen, and AppBrain.com.

debugging tests, and guides for creating apps for just about any purpose. Ultimately, you'll be able to reach millions of iPhone, iPad, and iTouch users via Apple's App Store.

BlackBerry OS Developer Zone: The BlackBerry platform supports several different ways to develop applications, mobile websites, themes, and even widgets. Each approach has its unique strengths, but all of them have the capability to leverage BlackBerry's key attributes, which are its connectivity and security. To distribute apps on BlackBerry's App World, you have to pay a fee for every 10 apps you submit for approval, but Black-Berry offers promotions to waive this fee on a regular basis.

Windows: The Windows platform may not be the world's largest, but its user interface is easy to use and, as a result, provides a solid user experience. The Windows Phone development program provides a lot of valuable documentation on the best practices for marketing your app. Plus, you don't have to worry about your app or game idea getting rejected after you've spent time creating it (a common criticism of Apple's approval process); Windows provides clear documentation on what will fly and what won't with its approval process.

The App Development Process for Ordinary Humans

What if you're not a programming junkie? What if you don't necessarily like to speak in code? Well, we have some good news: There are plenty of app development tools for ordinary humans, too.

AppMakr

This is a browser-based platform designed to make creating your own iPhone app quick and easy. You can use existing content and social networking feeds to produce a variety of different approaches for your app. It includes features such as push notifications, location-aware GeoRSS, custom CSS, and JavaScript capabilities. Some of the companies currently working with AppMakr include *Newsweek*, PBS *NewsHour* and *Inc*. magazine. The only downside is that, as of this writing, AppMakr works only on the iOS operating system.

GENWI

This tablet and smartphone publishing platform allows you to create and manage your presence on all popular mobile devices, including iPad, iPhone, Android, and HTML5 apps. It delivers rich graphics, photos, video, audio, and other forms of interactivity. And it enables you to revise your apps as often as you like. What's more, apps can also include various revenue-generating capabilities for businesses, like ads, coupons, and in-app subscriptions.

MIPPIN

One of the greatest strengths of the Mippin platform is its ease of use. It allows you to create apps for Android, iOS, and Windows, and provides you a good deal of flexibility in designing the app. You can even have Mippin distribute your app for you to the iTunes, Android, Windows, and Amazon stores.

MOBBASE

Are you a singer or in a band? If so, then MobBase is for you. This app builder allows you to use an RSS feed to keep your fans up to date on band news and events; lets you upload tracks for fans to listen to while browsing the apps; and even makes it easy for fans to find information on upcoming shows, buy tickets, and get directions. Move over, U2.

MOBICART

Do you have an e-commerce store that you'd like to take into the mobile sphere? Then MobiCart is just what you're looking for. MobiCart links up with PayPal to allow any business or consumer with an e-mail address to securely, conveniently, and cost-effectively send and receive payments online.

MYAPPBUILDER

For just $29 a month, MyAppBuilder will create an iPhone or Android app for you. All you have to do is provide content (videos, books, etc.) and their pros will take it from there. You don't need a technical background to develop an app with MyAppBuilder. They'll even take care of the hassle of uploading it to the app store for you.

RunRev

You can use RunRev's LiveCode to develop your app, which is an English-like language for developing iPhone and Android apps. With this cross-device platform, you can build live prototypes that use the full capabilities of iOS and Android devices and deploy to whatever platform your customers need. The site is also packed with plenty of tutorials to help you along the way.

ShoutEm

Another easy-to-use platform is available via ShoutEm, which is set up for bloggers, students, sports fans, news portals, and local publishers. You don't have to have knowledge of coding to set up your app, and ShoutEm will even take care of the iTunes and Android Marketplace submission process.

SwebApps

These guys provide a simple, inexpensive way to build, track, and update a native mobile app for your business. You create an iPhone and/or Android app online, and once it is available for download via the iTunes Store or Android Marketplace, you can update your content in real time through SwebApps. You'll have to make a small investment to go through SwebApps, but it's a small price to pay for what seems to be a very professional service, backed by people who know what they're doing.

Should You Build an App for Your Business?

In the end, apps can be a terrific way to differentiate your brand, to open up new revenue channels, and/or to deepen your relationship with your customers. But they're a bit of a challenge to create and produce if you're going to develop them yourself. An alternative is to use one of the plug-and-play systems mentioned in this chapter. Although they don't give you as much flexibility as you'd have if a developer created the app, they do provide simpler and easier ways to get an app built, approved, and running.

Do This:

- If you're developing an app yourself, be sure to budget a good amount of time and money for the development process.
- If you're using a plug-and-play system, be aware that you won't have as much flexibility as if you developed one yourself.
- Consider building a mobile website that has the look and feel of an app. It'll have the added benefit of not requiring a download for people to use it.

Don't Do This:

- Don't dive into the app process thinking you'll have one finished in a few hours. Even if you're using one of the simpler plug-and-play systems, it always helps to do some planning first.
- Don't think tactically. Instead, think strategically. What are your goals for your app? How are you going to measure whether it is successful? How will you calculate the ROI of your app?

Chapter 16

How to Use 2D Codes to Connect with Customers

There's a trick to using 2D codes that a lot of people overlook. Most businesses think the cool thing about 2D codes is that people can scan them and be instantly taken to a web page. But that's not the cool part. The cool part is what happens *after* people get to the web page, and that's where many businesses fall short.

Think of it this way: A TV, in and of itself, isn't really all that big a deal. It's the content you can access *through* the set that's the cool thing. The same holds true with 2D codes; it's what happens once you scan a 2D code that makes it a fun and engaging marketing tool.

2D codes have actually been around for quite some time. Bar codes, also known as 1D codes, were first developed 40 years ago to help track information about products. Then, in 1994, a subsidiary of Toyota called Denso Wave introduced the first 2D code as a way to track car parts in vehicle manufacturing. Denso Wave had a good deal of success with 2D codes, but they didn't cross into the mainstream for more than a decade after they were introduced.

Note: The term *2D code* is used to describe the category in general, not any specific type of code. Some of the most common types of 2D codes include Datamatrix, EZ Code, Microsoft Tag, QR codes, SPARQCode, and ScanLife, among others (see Table 16.1).

TABLE **16.1**   Common 2D Codes

	2D Code Format	Download Link*
SPARQCode	QR, UPC/EAN	SPARQ.it
BeeTagg Reader	QR, DataMatrix, BeeTagg	Get.BeeTagg.com
AT&T Code Scanner	QR, DataMatrix, UPC/EAN	Scan.Mobi
ScanLife	EZcode, QR, DataMatrix, UPC/EAN	GetScanLife.com
Microsoft Tag	Tag	GetTag.mobi

*If a 2D code reader isn't already installed on your phone, you can download one by visiting one of these websites from your mobile device.

A traditional 1D bar code stores up to 30 numbers, whereas a 2D code can store up to 7,089 numbers, which gives it the capability to store text, hyperlinks, telephone numbers, SMS messages, e-mails, vCards, or calendar entries. The capability to store hyperlinks means that visitors can do more than simply load a web page; they can play a video, download a mobile app, check in on foursquare, update their Twitter status, "like" a Facebook page, display map directions, or any number of other activities.

2D codes can be printed on just about any location or surface: newspapers, posters, TV ads, clothing labels, menus, even cake frosting. It's important to keep in mind that the location must be mobile-friendly—subways, elevators, and rural areas with bad cell coverage are not places to scan a 2D code.

Microsoft Tag, ScanLife, SPARQCode, and other 2D codes allow for data tracking. Some tools will track only the number of scans, while others provide detailed metrics like demographics, repeat scans, geolocation, and more.

2D codes also include an error correction function that makes it possible to scan "damaged" codes. The error tolerance level can be as high as 30 percent, which gives you creative license in developing designer 2D codes. Items like "jelly beans," "sand castles," and "product packaging" have even been used, because as long as there is enough contrast to read the code, the error correction function helps the scanning mechanism adapt to the inadequacies of the code.

FIGURE **16.1**   Want to give a 2D code a try? Just download a QR code reader from SPARQ.it, then scan this code. It'll take you to a blog post on the 60 Second Marketer mobile website called "101 Top Mobile Apps for Business."

How Businesses Are Using 2D Codes to Engage Customers

More than 25 percent of the Fortune 50 have already used 2D codes as a marketing tool.[1] Here are several of the best examples we've come across. You can use them for inspiration:

- *Real estate agents* are using 2D codes to provide drive-by visitors access to videos that show the insides of homes and other buildings. That way, interested parties can see the interiors without having to set up an appointment and wait to see them.
- *BestBuy* has added 2D codes to its in-store fact tags so that consumers can access information about its products. Customers can also opt to save the information for later review at home, or to buy the product instantly via smartphone and have it delivered to their homes at a later date/time.
- *Delta and other airlines* use 2D codes in conjunction with their mobile apps. Users receive their boarding passes via the apps and use the 2D code on the boarding pass to check in at the airport.
- *Trade shows, events, and conferences* are using 2D codes on name tags. Participants can scan the codes and download a person's contact information instantly. No more business card swapping.

- *Esquire Magazine* uses 2D codes to give readers more information about fashion items featured in the magazine. Users can link to a designer's website to place an order for a product they saw in the magazine.
- *The Good Cook* on BBC1 in the United Kingdom provides 2D codes so viewers can access an ingredients list and the cooking method used by the chef.
- *Hotels* provide 2D codes in rooms to highlight local attractions, along with coupons to theme parks and restaurants.
- *The U.S. Department of Transportation and the Environmental Protection Agency* are proposing 2D code fuel economy labels on the window of every new vehicle in dealer showrooms.
- *The New York Times Magazine* put a 2D code made entirely of balloons on the cover of the publication. Users who scanned the 2D code were driven to a special mobile web page promoting the magazine's "10th Annual Year in Ideas" issue.
- *McDonald's* uses 2D codes in Japan to provide additional product information and promotions for its menu items.
- *Bosch VitaFresh Refrigerators* in Germany placed oversized, wrapped packages of meat—purportedly from dinosaurs, mammoths, and saber-toothed tigers—in supermarket freezers. The 2D codes on the packages linked to product information about the company's refrigerators, resulting in more than 75,000 views from customers in stores.
- *A bank in Ireland* provided maps of the Emerald Isle to customers. The map referenced a list of restaurants from across the country. Each one featured a 2D code that drove people through a Google map of the restaurants' locations.
- *Bigmouthmedia* in Edinburgh, Scotland, includes a 2D code on its Google map location, which gives people searching for the firm regular computer access to its website via mobile, too.

2D Code Case Studies

One of the best examples of using 2D codes comes from the Smithsonian Institution in Washington, DC. The Smithsonian's Natural History Museum incorporated 2D codes into its Neanderthal exhibit.

Neanderthals were early humans who roamed the earth between 50,000 and 130,000 years ago, throughout Europe and parts of the Middle East, before being replaced by *Homo sapiens*—modern humans.

How to Generate Your Own 2D Code

If you do a search for "2D code generator," you'll find plenty of options. Alternatively, you can visit the 60 Second Marketer blog and scroll down to the bottom right-hand side of the page. There you'll find a 2D code generator that's quick and easy to use.

To help visitors learn about Neanderthals, the Natural History Museum created an exhibit called the Meanderthal exhibit—that's not a typo. It's very hard to walk by an exhibit with a 2D code and a placard asking you to take part in such an exhibit.

How did it work? Visitors were asked to scan the 2D code from their smartphones. The code drove them through to the Meanderthal website, where they were encouraged to take a photograph of themselves. The person's image would then have a Neanderthal's facial features superimposed over it, right there at the exhibit. In other words, old Uncle Bob could see immediately what he might have looked like as a cave man. (In truth, Uncle Bob already looks like a cave man, but you get our point.)

What made the exhibit even more fun was that it could go viral. Users were encouraged to share their Meanderthal images with friends and family via Facebook and Twitter. The result was that the Natural History Museum encouraged visitors to stay engaged with an exhibit for much longer than they ordinarily would have done. And because the images went viral, word about the exhibit spread around the world much more quickly than if it had been promoted via traditional marketing methods.

This brings us to the more important point we made at the beginning of the chapter: 2D codes aren't cool in and of themselves; they're cool because they drive you through to a bigger and better brand experience than otherwise would be possible.

Another example of an organization that does a good job with 2D codes is Six Star Pro Nutrition, a company that produces nutritional supplements for marathoners, weight lifters, and other athletes.

The challenge to Six Star is that nutritional supplements can often be confusing to people confronted with a wealth of options at their local vitamin store, grocery store, or Walmart. There are so many different brands to choose from, as well as a wide variety of different product options within each brand. All this can get pretty confusing.

Six Star Pro Nutrition turned the challenge into an opportunity, to differentiate its brand from the competition, by adding 2D codes to each of its product labels. The codes do more than just drive people through to a coupon or a regular mobile web page; they drive consumers through to simple, easy-to-use pages designed to help them figure out which product is best for their needs.

As a marathoner, do you want whey protein? Creatine? Or some other supplement? And when should you take your supplement? Before your run? After? Just scan the 2D code to find out. Or if you're a weight lifter, when should you use whey isolate? Casein protein? Or take a protein energy shot? Those are important questions for weight lifters interested in nutritional supplements. A simple scan of the 2D code drives them through to a page where they can further identify themselves as someone interested in preworkout products, postworkout products, protein products, and/or amino acid products.

In the end, Six Star Pro Nutrition differentiates its brand from others in the field by getting inside the minds of its prospects and figuring out what customers need at the moment they're scanning the 2D code. Six Star didn't simply default to a coupon or a promotional landing page. Instead, it analyzed customer behavior and recognized that such a wide variety of products might cause some confusion. The company then used that insight to design a 2D code campaign that answered consumers' questions, thereby deepening its relationship with both prospects and customers.

2D Code Best Practices

There are several factors to keep in mind when using 2D codes for marketing purposes.

1. *Provide clear instructions.* Just because you're familiar with 2D codes doesn't mean everybody is. Help your visitors along by providing them with a line of copy that explains what 2D codes are and how to use them. Here's some sample copy:

   > *Scan the 2D "code" to receive a special coupon. If you don't already have a code reader on your phone, open your mobile browser and visit SPARQ.it.*

2. *Drive visitors through to web pages designed specifically for smartphones.* This may seem obvious, but you'd be surprised how many companies drive people through to regular web pages that are hard to read on mobile phones. Remember, a good 2D code experience equals return visits, which is what you're looking for.

3. *Run your 2D code promotion in an area that has good cell phone coverage.* We discussed this earlier, but it's worth repeating: It's frustrating for customers to try and scan a code in an area with bad cell coverage. Fortunately, bad cell phone coverage is increasingly rare.

4. *Add value for your customer.* The best 2D code promotions give people something extra for their trouble. Sometimes, as in the case of the Meanderthal exhibit, it's an enhanced user experience. Other times, it's something as simple as a discount code or special coupon. The key is to reward customers for their time and trouble.

5. *Track your results.* Not every 2D code generator includes a tracking mechanism, but the best paid options do. If you're interested in tracking the results of your campaign, it's worth the investment. As we've said before, what's the point of running a 2D code campaign if you can't tell how many people scanned the code and, thus, how well the campaign worked?

6. *Conduct A/B split tests.* When you run a 2D code promotion, you'll often be driving visitors through to a mobile landing page. Why not test two different landing pages to see which one converts the best? Once you have a winner, use that

landing page as your control and see if you can beat the results with alternate landing pages.

7. *Keep your 2D code campaigns updated.* One of the advantages of 2D codes is that the landing pages can be updated on a regular basis. So, for example, if a grocery store has an in-store 2D code that says, "Scan here to get this week's discount," the grocery store can change the landing page every week to keep the promotion fresh. The in-store 2D code stays the same; only the landing page changes.

8. *Test before you deploy.* Test your 2D code off the final proof of the printed materials you're deploying. There's nothing worse than sending out thousands of posters with a 2D code only to find the wrong code was printed.

As with all mobile marketing techniques, your 2D code campaign will work best when it's integrated with other marketing programs. Resist the temptation to run your 2D code promotion in isolation. Instead, run it in tandem with your other campaigns. When you do so, you'll find your results will be much healthier.

The Future of 2D Codes

Will 2D codes be around forever? Nope. Will they be around for many years? Maybe. They're a terrific, fun tool you can use to effectively differentiate your brand; but newer technologies, like near field communications and Google Goggles, will probably replace 2D codes within a few years.

NFC technology enables businesses to connect with consumers using wireless communications. Consumers simply wave their phones in front of in-store posters or other media that have an NFC transmitter embedded into the advertisement.

As for Google, it recently worked with Buick, Disney, Diageo, T-Mobile, and Delta Airlines to create marketing materials that leveraged its Google Goggles technology. Users simply opened Google from their iPhone or Android devices and snapped a photograph of the ad. Google Goggles scanned the ads and drove consumers through to web pages that matched the content of the ads. In effect, it was as if the ad were a huge 2D code that didn't require installing special software to read it.

Does this mean 2D codes aren't worth the trouble? Not necessarily. For the time being, 2D codes are valuable tools. What we are saying is that within a few years, we expect 2D codes to be replaced by NFC technology and other tools like Google Googles.

Until then, use 2D codes as much as you can; they're a great way to help your company or brand stand out in a crowded marketplace.

Do This:
- ◆ Track the results of your mobile marketing campaign. When marketing campaigns are measured, they invariably improve.
- ◆ Be creative. It's frustrating for people scanning your code to be driven to a page with no special value or reward.
- ◆ Provide guidance for your consumers. Not everybody is 100 percent familiar with how to use 2D codes. Give them the help they need and your results will improve.

Don't Do This:
- ◆ Don't run your 2D code program in isolation. If you integrate the promotion with other marketing campaigns, your results will improve.

Note
1. www.burson-marsteller.com/Innovation_and_insights/blogs_and_pod casts/BM_Blog/Lists/Posts/Post.aspx?ID=243; accessed October 25, 2011.

Chapter 17

Tablet Computers

Taking the World by Storm

Tablet computing isn't all about Apple and the iPad. Okay, maybe it is. But it won't be that way forever; Google is making some inroads, and Amazon has introduced the Kindle Fire, which can do many things the iPad can do for significantly less money.

The very first versions of tablet computers were essentially small laptops with clunky user interfaces. Next came e-books, which didn't fully leverage the potential of a tablet computer. But then Steve Jobs and the other geniuses at Apple (and they really *are* geniuses) came along and reinvented the entire category.

The quantum leap in tablets wasn't just the touch screen, which was a technology already in use. The quantum leap was incorporating the use of GPS, a compass, a gyroscope, and an accelerometer into the units. By adding these capabilities to the tablet computing platform, a whole new world opened up.

For example, thanks to GPS capability, your tablet computer knows your location, which improves the entire user experience. If, say, you're using Yelp to look up reviews of nearby restaurants, the GPS lets the application know that you're standing on the corner of 53rd and 3rd in New York City. In addition, the compass knows that you're facing north while looking through the view screen on your tablet computer. Yelp puts the restaurant reviews in an overlay on the screen. In other words, right there—live—you can see arrows pointing to the restaurants that are on 3rd Avenue heading north in New York City. Better still, the arrows include user ratings, which give you an indication of the quality of the food you'll be served at each restaurant.

Gyroscopes are also an important part of the tablet experience because they enable the apps to understand how you're holding the tablet computer. Are you pointing it toward the sky? If so, then apps like Star Walk can superimpose the night sky on your screen, complete with stars, galaxies, and constellations. Just tap on the star, galaxy, or constellation and up pops information about each celestial entity. It's an amazing experience.

The accelerometers in tablet computers are also put to good use. The iPad has several pedometer apps that give you input on your average speed, calories burned, and distance walked. There's even a seismometer app that displays movement in all three dimensions as a dynamic graph. That app is ideal for university students and scientists, but it can also be used by parents who might, for example, place the tablet computer on their young child's bed so that it beeps if the child sleepwalks or otherwise gets out of bed.

In addition to GPS, a compass, a gyroscope, and an accelerometer, most tablets also have ambient light and proximity sensors. These give the tablets the capability to respond to user interaction by adjusting screen brightness, and make other changes based on the user's proximity to the screen.

Conversion Rate on Tablet Computers 50 Percent Higher Than on Desktops

According to a report from Forrester Research,[1] the conversion rate on tablet computers exceeds that on desktops by as much as 50 percent.

On traditional PCs, the percentage of people who visit an e-commerce site and actually buy a product hovers around 3 percent. For shoppers using tablets, that figure jumps to 4 or 5 percent.

Many retailers also report that tablet users tend to place bigger orders, in some cases adding 10 to 20 percent more to their orders. The reason is assumed to be because the typical tablet owner's household income is higher than that of the general population.

The bottom line is that tablet computers are transformational, and they're here to stay. For the foreseeable future, they will become an increasingly important part of our lives.

According to technology research firm Gartner, Inc.,[2] tablet sales are expected to experience strong growth through 2015, when sales are forecast to reach 326.3 million units. Apple's iPad accounts for about 75 percent of the worldwide tablet market, down slightly from a high of 83 percent. By 2014, Gartner predicts that Apple will still command more than 50 percent of the tablet computing market. That's *huge*. What company wouldn't want a 50 percent market share of a multibillion-dollar industry?

Android tablets account for about 18 percent of the current market, but according to Gartner, by 2015 they'll be approaching 40 percent market share. This means that unless things change dramatically, the tablet computer market will be dominated by Apple and Google for the foreseeable future.

Tablets versus Desktops and Laptops

When a new technology is adopted, it doesn't replace the previous technology as much as it *supplements* it. For example, when radio was introduced, it didn't replace newspapers; it was simply added to the existing pool of options. And when television came along, it didn't replace radio. Nor did PCs replace TVs.

Each new technology acts as a complement to the previous technology. And that holds true for table computers. They're not here to replace desktops and laptops; they're here to complement that experience.

In the B2B world, if a salesperson is having a discussion with a client and wants to review a spreadsheet, opening up a laptop, turning it on, and waiting for it to boot up is a laborious process. Not so with a tablet, which is as easy to turn on as it is to open a book. And even though most people think "app" when they think about tablets, the fact of the matter is they should be thinking "cloud." Cloud computing will allow people to carry tablets with them and instantly access information that's important to the success of their businesses.

Imagine you're working in a warehouse and need to access an inventory management system that tracks new shipment orders coming in. If you have to walk from the warehouse floor back to the office to check the spreadsheet before making a call to the delivery truck 90 minutes away, you're wasting a lot of time. With a portable tablet, you tap a screen, check the data, and click on your Bluetooth-enabled headset to call the truck driver.

Bingo.

Tablets Transform Teaching and Education

The immediacy of tablet computing offers numerous additional benefits. Doctors, nurses, and medical technicians are using tablets to monitor the health of their patients. They can help a patient under-stand a diagnosis, or be used to walk through a medical procedure or describe a therapy with them. Restaurants are using tablets as customer survey tools, or to enable patrons to review the menu prior to being seated.

But one of the most important and valuable uses of tablets will be in the field of education. Imagine a high school classroom where 24 percent of the students are visual learners, 24 percent are tactile learners, 24 percent are auditory learners, and 24 percent are verbal (written language) learners; 96 percent of the classroom is made up of four different styles of learners. (What about the other 4 percent? Nobody really knows because they're asleep in the back of the class.)

For centuries, teachers have been limited in their ability to transfer information to students because individuals process information so differently. If a student is a visual learner and the teacher spends most of the day at the front of the classroom communicating aurally, much of the information being shared by the teacher will be lost on that student.

Now imagine you're the teacher and that you have a tablet computer preloaded with information about Roman history. It enables you to teach a Roman history course complete with dynamic timelines, 3D renderings of buildings, and video animations of historic battles. It even features immersive hologram renderings of everyday life in Rome, allowing your students to move the tablet in a 360-degree circle and see what the city of Rome looked like in 33 AD.

You can imagine the impact this would have on your students. Today, most students are taught in a way that's not conducive to their cognitive learning styles. This is not a reflection on teachers, who work incredibly hard for very little pay; rather, it's a reflection on the inefficiencies that are an innate part of a system that has 1 teacher for every 25 or 30 students.

Think about the difference it would make if each student were provided with a tablet computer that allowed them to learn in their own style. In short, the impact on their learning would be monumental. More, the impact on *culture* would be monumental, because the education system would improve its teaching efficiencies dramatically.

Putting Tablet Computers to Work for You

The biggest challenge most businesses face today regarding tablet computing is that the handful of plug-and-play app development options don't fully leverage the capabilities of tablet computers. If you're looking for a straightforward tablet app, some of the plug-and-play app development platforms will get the job done, but you won't get a fully customized experience.

If, however, you want to create an app that leverages a tablet computer's GPS, compass, gyroscope, or accelerometer, you'll have to go directly to an app developer. In this case, it's always a good idea to use a developer who is in your market, as that will facilitate communication; but if you're willing to go outside of your market, you can use websites like ELance.com and AppMuse.com to generate bids on your project.

ELance and AppMuse are project-bidding aggregators that send your bids out to multiple prospects. Each prospect bids on the assignment and, by following a series of steps, you assign the final project to one of the bidders.

Tablet computers are still in their infancy. It was only a few short years ago that the iPad was introduced and revolutionized the tablet computing market. Even in that short time, tablet computing has evolved and changed dramatically. As the market continues to evolve, and as more consumers adopt the technology, the tablet computer will become a dominant player in the world of mobile marketing. They won't replace desktop models, but they'll certainly complement them. And as more bells and whistles are added to them (for example, wireless phone capabilities), more businesses will find innovative uses for these incredible, and incredibly convenient, devices.

Do This:
◆ Open your mind to the potential of tablet computers for businesses of all kinds. By leveraging the GPS, compass, gyroscope, and accelerometer capabilities, you'll be able to create apps that differentiate your brand and improve customer loyalty.

Don't Do This:
◆ Don't downplay the importance of tablet computers. A number of people were frustrated early on with the iPad because it didn't support Flash, and gave up on it. But they were in the minority. Don't be one of them in this case. Embrace the potential power of tablet computing and figure out how to leverage it for the good of your business.

Notes
1. www.qrcodepress.com/tablets-encourage-users-to-make-a-purchase/854352; accessed October 25, 2011.
2. www.gartner.com/it/page.jsp?id=1800514; accessed October 25, 2011.

Part IV

Expanding Your Horizons

Chapter 18

Using Mobile E-Commerce to Drive Revenue

As mobile computing usage continues to grow at a staggering rate, the number of consumers who are turning to their smartphones and handheld devices for all of their shopping needs is keeping pace. According to marketing research firm ABI Research, mobile commerce activity is projected to reach more than $119 billion annually by 2015.[1] Furthermore, more than half of all mobile phone sales in the United States are now smartphone devices.[2] These impressive numbers make it imperative for businesses of all kinds to begin developing a mobile e-commerce presence for their customers.

Mobile e-commerce, or *m-commerce* as it is sometimes called, is a relatively new phenomenon. Since its humble start in Europe just over a decade ago, the medium has quickly become one of the most lucrative avenues available for drawing in new customers and retaining existing shoppers. While many businesses had already begun experiencing a steady climb in active mobile shoppers, the growth explosion in the industry in recent years can largely be attributed to the advent of popular devices such as the Apple iPhone and Android-powered phones. Today, some companies are pulling in massive amounts of revenue through mobile sales, including eBay, which posted global mobile sales of nearly $2 billion last year alone.[3]

Whereas previously some consumers expressed concern about the safety of conducting shopping transactions via their mobile devices, technological advances and safeguards introduced by many mobile retailers have all but eliminated any lingering doubts about the legitimacy of mobile sales. In fact, many consumers now expect their favorite brands and businesses to offer mobile shopping options. Development of such shopping opportunities is no longer regarded as a simple extra feature for retailers to offer; rather, the implementation of a mobile processing system is considered almost an obligatory part of doing business effectively.

Mobile sales largely take place in two different ways. The first, and by far the most common, is through a web browser. Shoppers either browse to your site directly, or are directed to your products through a search engine query. The purchase is made by selecting the product(s) desired, and then entering in payment and shipping information. In an effort to streamline the entire process, many companies have begun offering customers the opportunity to store their sensitive details remotely, making the need to enter specific information for each purchase obsolete.

Dollars Spent via Mobile Devices

According to Forrester Research, nearly $150 billion was spent online in the United States last year, of which 3 percent came via mobile devices.[4]

While only 9 percent of online shoppers own tablets computers, the conversion rate from tablet computers is nearly 50 percent higher than on regular desktops.

Shopping network QVC likes the concept of mobile e-commerce so much, it encourages tablet use on-air and via its social media channels. According to the *Salt Lake Tribune*, mobile commerce accounts for about 3 percent of QVC's revenue.[5]

When mobile e-commerce first began to gain popularity, many companies, in an effort to keep pace, simply made certain that their websites were compatible with the browsers of mobile devices. For many brands, that meant removing complicated Adobe Flash components and scripting from their sites' main pages. Additional adjustments potentially included simplifying the site navigation structure and replacing antiquated text with mobile-friendly fonts.

Today, merely adjusting one's website is no longer seen as a viable solution for courting mobile customers. Instead, many companies have developed mobile versions of their websites that can recognize the mobile device an Internet consumer is using to view their content. When a mobile device or smartphone is identified, the user is routed to the mobile page.

As the smartphone craze has gained ground across the globe, the second option for mobile e-commerce sales has developed: *dedicated applications*. Apps are powerful tools for online retailers, as they are developed for optimal display on the device used to view the content, and they provide consumers with a direct and ever-present link to a company's products. Popular app databases, such as the Android Market and Apple's App Store, are now filled with apps from both small and large retailers alike.

The sheer rise in the number of consumers using smartphones is largely responsible for the incredible growth of the mobile app marketplace. According to market researcher IHS, global mobile app sales for 2011 are slated to reach a massive $4 billion, which does not take into account the huge number of free apps available, including most mobile e-commerce applications.[6] The Apple App Store alone reached an incredible 10 billion downloads earlier this year, a number that continues to climb daily.[7]

In addition to improving overall sales performance, the development of dedicated mobile applications has proven to be an effective tool for expanding the breadth of a brand's influence. One of the ways this is accomplished is by providing consumers with a polished and user-friendly shopping avenue that is enjoyable to use. Customers who have already visited a physical retail store and had a positive experience there are more likely to attempt to purchase products from the same company online (see Figure 18.1). An effective app will allow consumers to make their purchases with ease, further cementing the relationship between them and the company in question.

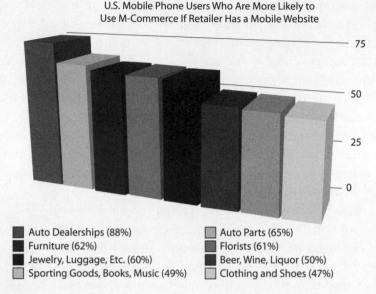

U.S. Mobile Phone Users Who Are More Likely to
Use M-Commerce If Retailer Has a Mobile Website

■ Auto Dealerships (88%)　　　■ Auto Parts (65%)
■ Furniture (62%)　　　　　　 ■ Florists (61%)
■ Jewelry, Luggage, Etc. (60%)　■ Beer, Wine, Liquor (50%)
□ Sporting Goods, Books, Music (49%)　□ Clothing and Shoes (47%)

FIGURE 18.1　The majority of consumers are ready, willing, and able to use m-commerce—provided the retailer has the capability to meet their needs. *Source:* Brand Anywhere and Luth Research, Supply & Demand of the Mobile Web for Retail, Nov 16, 2010.

If you are looking to build your own mobile web presence, there are several fundamental ideas you will want to take advantage of in order to make your launch into the mobile world as successful as possible. Not only will the development of a dedicated mobile app or mobile site encourage the growth of another lucrative sales avenue, but such a tool can help to improve sales in your physical retail locations. Use the key ideas in the following subsections to start your endeavor off on the right foot.

Develop a Marketing Strategy

Developing a marketing strategy is one of the most important steps when establishing a mobile e-commerce platform. Rather than focusing entirely on the development of the specific app or browser-based shopping platform, it is important to begin your quest to enlarge your brand's scope by determining who it is you intend to target, and how you will reach those individuals effectively. You also need to take the specific medium, mobile computing, into account.

Require a Level of Personal Commitment from Mobile Users

People are more likely to develop an attachment to something that they've had to sacrifice for. Therefore, one way to strengthen brand loyalty in your mobile customers is to ask them to make a small sacrifice in order to receive a reward from your company. Cereal companies have used this tactic for years; they encourage children to collect box tops, for example, to send away for trinkets, or to find a "secret code" to access online games.

You can use this tactic with your mobile users. Ask them to register to gain access to certain apps or coupons. Make some deals contingent upon texting to a certain number, or logging in to the mobile website for a week straight. Or, if you have branded games for mobile phones, link certain scores to privileges on the mobile site. If you merely give customers a 20 percent off coupon, they may ignore it and pass up an opportunity to try one of your new products. If, instead, they "earn" it by playing a game, it will seem like a prize, and they'll be more likely to use it.

Many marketers don't understand that the mobile e-commerce world is not a carbon copy of its big brother, the desktop e-commerce industry, in miniature form. Mobile phone users do not browse the web in the same way you can expect a consumer sitting in front of a home computer to do so. Rather, mobile computing sessions are generally shorter in length than those on their desktop counterparts. Furthermore, many consumers will likely visit your mobile platform for the sole purpose of purchasing goods, rather than "window shopping" for fun. Thus, you must pay careful attention to the navigation and structure of the overall platform, to ensure that it is conducive to consumers looking to make their purchases as quickly as possible, regardless whether the platform in question is a mobile website or an app.

Narrowing down the target group will help you to determine which tasks need to be most accessible on the mobile e-commerce platform. For example, if your primary concern is expanding sales and influence by pulling in new shoppers, you will want to spend time formulating a specific plan to reach those consumers. Will you invest in mobile advertising to draw them to your site? Perhaps you should spend some time developing partnerships with other companies in your field?

Once you have established an effective way to reach those customers, you will need to tailor the app or mobile site to meet their specific needs. A new customer may want to learn more about your brand and discover where you are located. Make it easy to access store information, including locations and operating hours.

On the contrary, if your primary concern is further developing the existing relationship between your brand and your customers, you will likely want to make supplementary information the most prevalent content on your mobile e-commerce platform. This may include details about previous purchases, which can be archived by developing online customer accounts. Customer service and contact options should also be displayed prominently. Remember, by establishing multiple channels of communication with your customers, you will be able to keep your brand accessible and relevant across the board.

Consider Expanding with Discounts and Deals

Increasing both sales figures and customer loyalty can easily be accomplished by providing your customers with discounts and deals for your merchandise. Whether you choose to offer these discounts and deals both in-store and online or in only one medium, the development of such money-saving opportunities is an effective way to pull in more traffic. Many companies have begun to offer mobile discounts that are applicable only to purchases made from the mobile device. Others use popular location-based social networking tools like foursquare and Gowalla to provide their customers with discounts once they have checked in at their stores on their mobile devices.

Establishing brand loyalty is no laughing matter. According to consulting firm Baines and Company, retaining a mere 5 percent of your customers can translate to increased profitability of 75 percent.[8] Securing brand loyalty through mobile discounts is not only easy to implement, it has proven effective for many companies seeking to improve their retention rates.

In addition to temporary deals and discounts, membership programs can play a significant role in customer retention and brand loyalty. While these programs are certainly not a new phenomenon in the retail world, their transition to the mobile e-commerce platform has not necessarily been a direct trajectory. Many companies are still torn about how best to implement their loyalty cards and membership plans into their mobile platforms; but one thing is clear: allowing web users to take advantage of these benefits when shopping on a mobile platform can be a powerful way to harness the power of membership groups, regardless of whether or not a customer visits your physical store.

Utilize Customer Knowledge and Experience

Companies that have a difficult time developing their mobile content often share their frustrations regarding uncertainty as to what their customers would like to see represented on a mobile platform. Rather than simply making guesses about what could potentially prove a lucrative option to explore, why not instead simply ask your customers what they would like to see represented on a mobile platform? Not only will this allow you to establish a useful solution for customers, it may give you valuable insight into how your existing customer base thinks and shops.

Asking your customers for their thoughts and opinions can be done in several different ways. Some retailers opt to use focus groups, either in person or online, which can prove effective for delving deeply into the perspectives of a select group of consumers. If, on the other hand, you would rather examine a wide swath of consumer perspectives, it might be a better idea to utilize surveys or customer comment cards for gleaning constructive ideas from those individuals. Some companies choose to focus on several different areas at once, in turn ensuring that they receive a thorough and comprehensive set of information.

Drive Existing Customer Adoption

Once a mobile solution has been developed, existing customers need to be encouraged to explore the different possibilities that are available in a mobile format. Your customers are likely wondering why they should take the time to adopt a mobile shopping solution, which is a question that you will be tasked with answering. The answer will vary greatly, depending once again on who you are targeting with the development of the application or mobile site.

This is where many companies choose to implement discounts and incentives. Beyond in-store and online savings, however, you may wish to expand in unique ways that will help your customers to feel better connected to your store. Establishing a sense of exclusiveness can accomplish incredible results when attempting to build brand loyalty.

One great example is to use your mobile platform to reveal upcoming product lines or shifts in your brand's direction. By sharing intimate details with your mobile customers, you can foster a rapport between them and your company. That rapport can lead to greater retention, by transforming everyday shoppers into loyal customers who will frequent your stores again and again.

■■■

While there is no perfect formula companies can follow to build effective mobile e-commerce solutions for their customers, creating a dynamic platform that they will enjoy using does not have to seem like mission impossible. By setting firm expectations and goals regarding the direction of your company's mobile platforms, you will be able to reach a maximum number of individuals. Furthermore, investing the necessary time and resources needed to develop a well-designed and useful mobile presence will ensure that your foray into mobile e-commerce is as successful as possible.

Do This:
- Create a sense of community to build brand loyalty.
- Listen to your customers for thoughts on products and services.

Don't Do This:

◆ Don't assume that mobile customers have different desires and needs from the general population. Given the current marketing penetration of mobile devices, they *are* the current population.

Notes

1. www.abiresearch.com/press/1605-Shopping+by+Mobile+Will+Grow+to+119+Billion+in+2015; accessed October 23, 2011.
2. www.smartonline.com/mobile-2/us-smartphone-statistics-q1–2011-overview; accessed October 23, 2011.
3. http://techcrunch.com/2011/01/06/ebay-mobile-sales-2010; accessed October 23, 2011.
4. www.mobilecommercedaily.com/2011/06/20/mobile-commerce-sales-to-reach-10-billion-next-year-forrester; accessed October 23, 2011.
5. www.sltrib.com/sltrib/money/52652268–79/tablets-tablet-percent-retailers.html.csp; accessed October 23, 2011.
6. www.computerworld.com/s/article/9217885/Your_next_job_Mobile_app_developer; accessed October 23, 2011.
7. www.appleinsider.com/articles/11/01/14/apple_begins_countdown_to_10_billion_app_store_downloads.html; accessed October 23, 2011.
8. www.rocketmarketinggroup.com/tag/customer-loyalty-statistics; accessed October 23, 2011.

Chapter 19

Mobile Marketing for B2B Companies

When a B2B enterprise is launching mobile marketing initiative, the first major step is to create a mobile marketing plan. During the planning process, many business leaders often have more questions than answers on how to tackle this new and exciting project. Some companies may take a very cautious and conservative approach to mobile marketing, while others may want to "go all the way" without first identifying the right approach for their particular business.

Getting Off to the Right Start

Before diving in too deep, here are six key questions to ask and answer, to help you get off to the right start with your B2B mobile marketing strategy:

1. *Why should I care about mobile marketing for B2B now?* The mobile arena is new and fresh, which gives businesses an opportunity to capitalize on the trend before it becomes mainstream. Companies that are early adopters of mobile marketing have an edge—they can get in front of their B2B customers ahead of their competition. Also, mobile marketing

is new, but not to the point of being too risky. The trend line is extremely positive for those who enter now, versus the pioneers who first ventured into mobile a year or so ago.

2. *This is just another marketing channel; it really doesn't replace any initiatives that businesses use currently, right?* Many businesses may consider this just another channel to leverage for marketing campaigns, but a paradigm shift is taking place, and companies need to be aware that many "stationary" PCs, and even televisions, are being replaced by smartphones and tablets. Your company should be aware that, very possibly, inside of a decade, desktop PCs will be obsolete. Thus, websites that were once visited regularly by PC and laptop users should be redesigned for such mobile devices as smartphones and tablets. The timeliness of your online updates need to be almost instant, or in real time— daily or weekly won't cut it anymore. Your web-based marketing channel could very quickly transform into *just* mobile marketing.

3. *Are B2Bs really using mobile today?* Businesses are indeed using mobile technology, and the use rate is growing exponentially. According to Morgan Stanley, mobile web use will be larger than desktop Internet use by 2015.[1] Gartner estimates that mobile devices will overtake PCs as the most common web devices by 2013.[2] With an estimated 4.5 billion mobile users today, B2B use cannot be ignored. Add to this the simple logic that businesspeople travel from town to town, customer to customer, meeting to meeting. Mobile is what B2Bs do—all day long. Marketing for mobile devices just makes logical sense for B2Bs.

4. *What are sound B2B mobile marketing approaches that really work?* Mobile techniques that work well today include region-specific information and alerts, immediate notification of order status, replenishment reminders, updates on new products or services, and announcements of sales specials or coupons. Businesses also have had great success with presentation deliveries, trade show campaigns, customer service requests, and event notifications.

Mobile Is Not Channel

Mobile is really a series of platforms that allow for on-the-go communications through SMS, apps, and social media networks, such as Facebook and Twitter, as well as e-mail.

When developing your mobile strategy, consider that smartphones are driving the increased utilization of major components of your online marketing program.

5. *Will business customers be ready?* Through your web analytics program, you can view current metrics on the type of device that is being used to visit your business websites. The odds are very good that a significant number of Androids, iPhones, and iPads are directed at your website now, so your mobile business users are probably more ready than you may think.

6. *What key elements should be part of a B2B mobile marketing plan?* Establish a vision/mission/goal statement for your mobile marketing strategy. Research and then decide which mobile marketing approaches to implement first. Include in the plan metrics on how to measure success. Allow for flexibility and adaptability—with rapidly changing technology, it is important to try new approaches and keep the content and campaigns fresh. Review the plan regularly; monthly, at the very least.

Businesses should always have an established plan, with overarching vision and mission statements. The mobile marketing plan should keep the overall corporate vision and mission in mind so that technology is not implemented just for the sake of the technology. This powerful medium of mobility should have a purpose, one founded within the corporate plan.

For businesses, putting together a solid B2B mobile marketing strategy can be quite challenging, especially in the face of evolving mobile technologies and the rapid adoption of new marketing methods, along with alternate communications channels. Nevertheless, businesses should not ignore the huge potential that exists to capitalize on the mobile communications evolution. With so many users trending toward mobile so quickly, businesses would be wise to stay on top of this wave of innovation, in order to leverage it to meet their sales and marketing goals.

Get Started: 10 Steps to B2B Mobile Marketing

1. *Identify your goals.* As with any aspect of business, it will be difficult to choose effective advertising solutions or measure the success of your campaigns without knowing what, specifically, you wish to accomplish. Are you looking to increase user engagement with your firm or sales representatives? Do you want to drive business to a physical location or online store? Strengthen a brand name? Update customers on new products? All of these goals can be accomplished using mobile, but choosing the right method(s) requires a specific plan.

2. *Choose the type of advertisement.* Mobile advertising comes in as many shapes and colors as traditional advertising options (if not more). Choose the type of ad carefully, to maximize its value to your business. If you are trying to sell a particular product, or advise users of a coupon, a mobile SMS ("text") campaign could be an excellent solution. On the other hand, a video would be a better way to demonstrate new product features to clients.

3. *Make your content relevant.* One of the great advantages of mobile advertising over traditional methods is the ability to specifically target users who would be interested in or benefit from your products and services. For example, suppose you owned an engineering consulting company that specialized in improving certain manufacturing operations. You might assume your business isn't well suited to mobile advertising; but if you associated your mobile marketing plan with certain sites (e.g., manufacturing blogs) or search terms (e.g., common problems you specialize in solving), you may find it more effective than any other marketing you engage in.

    On the other hand, the opposite holds equally true: B2B mobile marketing that is not related to the content the user is interacting with is, quite frankly, a waste of your valuable advertising dollars.

4. *Make your content interactive.* When you consider the amount of rich, dynamic content available on the Internet, it makes sense that users are generally uninterested in flat, noninteractive ads. A mobile campaign that actively solicits engagement from the user in some manner (a survey, a response, a video) not only helps you measure the effectiveness of your advertising (more on that later), but makes it more likely your content will leave an impression on the user. Great mobile marketing can blur the line between advertising and entertainment.

5. *Tailor the experience to mobile users.* It may seem simple, but this is by far the worst mistake made by companies using mobile marketing strategies. If the advertisement or application you're using has a phone number listed, users should be able to tap it on their smartphones and place a call. If you are trying to direct customers to a store, there should be a handy map or link to navigation tools. If users click on a link, make sure it's optimized for mobile, so they aren't dealing with a slow-loading site.

6. *Use better metrics.* In the past, all online marketing has seemingly been based on one metric: total clicks generated. While this is still a prevalent metric, mobile, especially B2B mobile marketing, should use a broader range of metrics to gauge effectiveness. For example, how long did a user engage with the content? How many views or clicks actually led to downloads, orders, or inquiries? For many B2B companies, a high level of engagement is much more important than an impressive number of clicks.

7. *Specialize your targets.* The rich data that can be mined from mobile marketing can be hugely advantageous—*if* you use it properly. Take the information mined from your audience to create subgroups. For example, if you're running an SMS campaign, make note of the users who respond and hone future campaigns toward them; this will increase your effectiveness while avoiding ill will among users who are unlikely to respond anyway.

8. *Find the right placement.* There are a wide variety of mobile marketing networks that will help you find placements and target your mobile marketing campaign, including Apple iAd, Google AdMob, Jumptap, and Mojiva. Choosing one, or even a variety, of these networks to guide you in placing your ads will help generate the best results. In addition, doing so will allow you to compare various networks and placements and determine what works and what doesn't.

9. *Think local.* Studies have found that mobile users are much more likely to be searching for local results than are desktop users. Consider focusing your efforts on specific locations. That may mean just the city your firm is based in; or it could mean creating a variety of smaller campaigns capable of focusing on local areas.

10. *Adapt, adjust, advance.* As with any kind of marketing, B2B mobile marketing requires you to make adjustments to maximize the effectiveness of your campaign. One of the best features of mobile marketing, however, is the instantaneous feedback available. Monitor your campaigns, adjust the strategy to make sure you're meeting your goals, and continue to advance your mobile marketing efforts.

Small Business Considerations

It is possible, as a small business owner, you already use smartphones and other mobile technology daily. If so, you can think about using these devices to produce a low-cost, highly effective, B2B marketing campaign. Here's how.

ACCENTUATE THE POSITIVE

Focus your B2B mobile marketing campaign on your strengths as a small business. Are you known for your excellent customer care? Use mobile to provide even better service. Allow customers to text you questions. You'll be able to respond quickly—from anywhere.

Instruct your customer service staff to encourage customers to send photos and videos. The visuals will help with trouble-shooting and give your company a reputation for being service-oriented and tech-savvy.

Develop an app to give your customers daily updates on your company and merchandise. Until recently, developing custom apps meant hiring programmers. Today, sites like Conduit let amateurs build and customize apps. To publicize your app, send a direct mail or promotional e-mail with a QR code to your clients. When they scan the code, it will automatically download your app to their smartphones.

Plan to advertise your B2B mobile marketing campaign through nonmobile means. You need to reach your customers and tell them that you're open to mobile contacts.

MAKE PERSONAL CONTACT

According to a recent Pew study, 58 percent of adults send and receive text messages on a regular basis.[3] Many adults now prefer texting because it is less disruptive and time-intensive than phone or e-mail.

Keep a mobile contact list, with notes on client needs. Text each client two or three times a month to touch base and give updates. You'll be able to maintain a close relationship and build brand loyalty with only a small effort.

Mobile-friendly also puts a human face on your small business. Upload a short video to YouTube each week, highlighting an aspect of your business. Keep it under two minutes so your customers can view it on their smartphones.

UPDATE FREQUENTLY

Make sure that your company blog is easy to read on a mobile phone, and update it frequently. Post updates on your products, news articles related to your industry, and corporate milestones.

To reach an even larger mobile audience, start a Twitter feed. Mobile users like Twitter because it is low-bandwidth, loads quickly, and displays well on all types of phone.

SOLICIT FEEDBACK

Before you roll out your B2B mobile marketing campaign, test each part on a variety of mobile devices. Even if your website, SMS, and apps work when you use them, expect some of your customers to experience problems. Solicit feedback on how your marketing is affecting your customers. Are they sharing your posts, videos, and tweets with colleagues at other companies? Have they downloaded your free app? Use customer feedback to fine-tune your campaign.

Venturing into the realm of mobile marketing while the competition is still scarce may be one of the best moves you will ever make for your small business. In addition to having the time to establish an authoritative presence before everyone else jumps on the bandwagon, you will also have time to experiment and get the feel for what does and does not work, to avoid little mistakes that will hand your next sale to the competition.

Do This:

- Be sure to think about your goals and objectives prior to launching a B2B mobile marketing campaign. It's much easier to arrive at a destination when you have a sense of where you are going.
- Track the results of your campaign. Marketing programs that are measured tend to improve. More important, tracking your results means you can calculate whether your campaign had a positive ROI. (See Chapter 20 for more information on this.)

Don't Do This:

- Don't assume that mobile marketing is a waste of time for B2B companies. The truth is it can be even more effective because a B2B company that's using mobile marketing sets itself apart from most of its competitors. Being different is good, especially in business.

Notes

1. http://mashable.com/2010/04/13/mobile-web-stats; accessed October 23, 2011.
2. www.mediapost.com/publications/article/120590; accessed October 23, 2011.
3. www.pewinternet.org/Reports/2010/Cell-Phone-Distractions/Major-Findings/1-Texting-while-driving.aspx; accessed October 23, 2011.

Chapter 20

How to Measure the ROI of Your Mobile Marketing Campaign

Mobile marketing is an exciting new opportunity. As we've mentioned, it's a transformative technology, one that ultimately is going to have greater impact than the advent of radio, TV, and the PC combined.

One of the more exciting aspects of mobile marketing is that it's *digital*. Why is this exciting? Because, as we pointed out earlier in *Go Mobile*, things that are digital are measurable, and things that are measurable invariably improve. In other words, because you can track data from your mobile marketing campaign, you can measure its effectiveness. And when you measure its effectiveness, you can work to improve your results.

The challenge most people have with this practice is that they don't know how to convert mobile data into information that tells them whether they have a positive return on investment (ROI). For example, they might be tracking visits to their mobile landing page, and they might even be tracking conversions on those landing pages, but they don't know how to take those metrics and convert them into one that tells them whether or not they're generating a positive ROI from their campaigns.

Mobile ROI Starts with Customer Lifetime Value

If you're going to track the ROI from your mobile marketing campaign, the key formula you'll need to know is the customer lifetime value formula (CLV). CLV, in its most fundamental sense, is the amount of revenue the average customer generates for your company during the time he or she remains a customer. Let's say you own a pest control company and you know that your average customer spends $100 per month for your services. If your typical customer stays with you for three years before he or she stops using your service, to calculate this metric, you'd take your monthly revenue per customer of $100 and multiply that by 36 months (3 years): $100 $\times$ 36 months, to arrive at a CLV of $3,600.

It's important to note that the formula we're using here is a very *basic* version of CLV. When you go deeper into the world of CLV, you start factoring in information like labor costs for servicing that customer, or the time value of money during that three-year period. But for our purposes, this formula is all we need to begin calculating the ROI from a mobile marketing campaign.

Putting the Customer Lifetime Value Formula to Work for You

The customer lifetime value formula can be used across a wide variety of industries. For example, if you're a tax accountant and you charge $1,000 to prepare the average tax return, and most of your clients stay with you for six years, then your CLV is $6,000.

CLV can work for real estate agents, attorneys, insurance agents, automobile manufacturers, mobile phone carriers, cable companies, even interior designers. Likewise, it works for a variety of brick-and-mortar retailers. For example, if your business is an auto repair shop and you know that the typical repair costs $500, and that the average customer comes back three times before he or she stops using your services, then your CLV is $1,500. Or, if you run a restaurant and the average ticket is $80 and the typical customer comes back five times before he or she stops showing up, then your CLV is $400.

Customer Lifetime Value Worksheet

Here's a simple worksheet you can use to calculate your customer lifetime value:

Average Revenue per Customer $ _____

Average Number of Repeat Visits per Customer _____

CLV = _____

If you don't already know your CLV, take a minute or two right now to figure it out. Even if you have to make a few assumptions, do so, as it will give you at least a baseline of the CLV for your business.

Once you've calculated your CLV, you'll want to figure out how much you'd have to spend to *acquire* a new customer. This is called your *cost of customer acquisition* (COCA). It's essentially the amount of money you're willing to spend to "capture" a new customer.

Many businesses allocate about 10 percent of their customer lifetime value for their cost of customer acquisition. Going back to the pest control example, we've established that its CLV is $100 per month × 12 months × 3 years = $3,600. If the firm allocated 10 percent of that as its allowable cost of customer acquisition, it'd have $360 to spend on advertising and marketing for every new customer acquired. That includes direct mail costs, paid search costs, banner ad costs—whatever. But as long as the firm could capture a new customer for every $360 spent, it would be meeting its COCA goal of $360 per customer.

The 10 percent figure for cost of customer acquisition is a rule of thumb. Some industries allocate only 5 percent as a COCA; other industries allocate 15 percent. But generally speaking, as a starting point, you should budget about 10 percent of your customer lifetime value as your cost of customer acquisition.

If you want to get more advanced, you can take your customer lifetime value and break it out on an item-by-item basis. In this case, for example, 10 percent of your CLV might be used for marketing (your COCA), 40 percent for labor costs, 30 percent for overhead, and 20 percent for your profit. When you start analyzing your business using the CLV formula, you'll have a better handle on whether or not your marketing program is generating a positive ROI.

Calculating the ROI of Your Mobile Marketing Campaign

Now that you know how to calculate your customer lifetime value and your allowable cost of customer acquisition, how do you use those figures to calculate the ROI of your mobile marketing campaign?

The best way is to slice off part of your existing marketing budget and allocate it to mobile. Let's say the pest control company traditionally uses direct mail and direct response television (DRTV) to acquire new customers. If it spends $2 million a year on a direct mail and DRTV, and its cost of customer acquisition is $360, then it should generate 5,555 new customers a year from its efforts. This would be pretty easy to track, because direct mail and DRTV can have tracking codes tied to them, as follows:

Budget for direct mail and DRTV = $2,000,000

CLV = $3,600

Allowable COCA = $360

New customer acquisitions based on marketing spend ($2M/ $360) = 5,555

How do we take these figures and use them to track and calculate the ROI of your mobile marketing campaign? It's easy; just slice off a segment of your current budget and use it for your mobile marketing campaign.

As an example, let's take 20 percent of the pest control company's $2 million direct mail and DRTV budget. That amount would be $400,000. We know from previous experience that spending $400,000 in direct mail and DRTV will generate 1,111 new customers for the company. If we were to allocate $400,000 to a mobile marketing campaign for the pest control company, we'd expect to acquire the same number of new customers (1,111) as a result of a mobile marketing campaign. Think about it: If it costs $360 for the pest control company to acquire a new customer, then in an ideal world it shouldn't matter whether that $360 was spent in direct mail, DRTV, or mobile marketing.

Let's take another look at the facts and figures around the pest control example before we move on:

Budget for direct mail and DRTV = $2,000,000

Customers acquired from direct mail and DRTV ($2M/$360) = 5,555

20 percent of overall budget redirected to mobile = $400,000

New customer acquisitions from mobile marketing spend = 1,111

Of course, there's always the chance that if you spend $400,000 on your mobile marketing campaign, it would exceed expectations. Instead of generating 1,111 new customers, it might generate 1,500 new customers. But the odds of that happening are not likely. After all, this is your first mobile marketing campaign and the chances of you hitting a grand slam home run right out of the box are pretty slim. A more likely scenario is that your mobile marketing campaign would generate fewer than 1,111 new customers—say, somewhere around 900 new customers.

Should you cancel your mobile marketing campaign because it only generated 900 new customers, instead of the 1,111 you could have acquired using direct mail and DRTV? Nope. As we mentioned, you won't hit a grand slam the first time at bat. You'll be lucky to hit a double. But if the campaign looks like it might have some viability, then you'll be able to test your way into success. You'll be able to eliminate the aspects of the campaign that underperformed and transfer that budget to aspects of the campaign that met expectations or overperformed.

Media Neutral

The best marketing campaigns are *media neutral*, which means there's no bias toward one medium or another. In a media-neutral campaign, each medium is measured to track its effectiveness. If one medium (e.g., radio) underperforms versus another medium (e.g., paid search), then the budget for the first medium would be cut and that money would be used in other, better-performing media. In other words, the money would be moved out of radio and into paid search.

For instance, if you used paid search, display ads, and SMS for your pest control mobile marketing campaign and found that paid search worked well, SMS was breakeven, and display was a failure, then you'd drop the display campaign and redirect that money into your paid search campaign. This is called being *media neutral* and it's a great way to improve the efficiencies of any marketing program.

How to Track Your Conversions with Mobile Marketing

We've reviewed a lot of different mobile marketing tools so far in *Go Mobile*. Some of them, like mobile apps and a mobile website, are usually used for branding purposes. They're important because they facilitate an emotional connection with prospects and customers; but they aren't always used to track the movement of prospects as they travel down the sales funnel.

Other mobile tools, like SMS, MMS, display ads, paid search, location-based marketing, and 2D codes, are better suited to track the journey people take from being a prospect to becoming a customer. The key is to set up your campaign so that it can be measured. By incorporating different tracking mechanisms into each tool, you'll be able to effectively measure the ROI of your overall mobile marketing campaign.

This is pretty easy to do with SMS and MMS. When users opt in to participate in an SMS or MMS campaign, they give you data that you can use to track their purchases with your brand. Let's assume you own a bookstore and want to encourage people to stop by your location to buy a book called, say, *Go Mobile*, then you'd send an SMS or MMS message like the following to your opt-in database: "*Go Mobile* is considered the *War and Peace* of business books. Readers weep with joy over its sizzling content. To get a 10 percent discount on your copy, use discount code 12345 at the cash register."

As vast numbers of people begin to purchase the book, you'll be able to track the redemptions of that discount code. And since demand will be so high for this particular book, the ROI of the campaign will be stratospheric.

In similar fashion, if yours is a B2B company and you want to track inbound leads, you might develop a mobile paid search campaign. Let's say you have a computer repair company and you want to generate leads from people who are having computer problems. The first thing you'd do is to set up a mobile paid search campaign that targets people in your local area who are searching for "computer repair." Then you'd create a mobile landing page that provides a quick summary of your expertise, a map of your location, a click-to-call phone number, plus a discount code that's unique to that campaign.

When users click on your mobile paid search ad, they're driven to your landing page. They'll use the phone number provided to call you to set up an appointment. You'll capture the discount code they're using so that you can track which campaign was used to acquire that customer. By tracking your results to this level of detail, you'll be able to determine which campaign is most effective; this then gives you the ability to improve your results over time.

Another example of a mobile marketing campaign that would be highly measurable is a mobile display campaign for a car dealership. As a car dealer, you're interested in attracting prospects who are actively searching for a new or used car. A great place to start would be to run a mobile display ad campaign on a mobile website such as *Car & Driver*'s. The ad would be tied directly to a promotion.

For example, it might read: "$500 Rebate on All New Lexus Convertibles." Prospects who clicked on the display ad would be driven to a landing page that was specific to the $500 rebate promotion. People who visited the landing page could be given a specific code to use at the dealership. By giving them a specific tracking code, you'd be able to tell how many customers bought a car by initially clicking through on the display ad.

Using Your Conversion Rate to Track Your Mobile ROI

When prospects click through to your landing page, they don't automatically become customers. In fact, the vast majority of them *don't* become customers. Just because 1,000 people clicked through to your landing page doesn't mean you acquired 1,000 new customers. Statistically speaking, if 1,000 people clicked through to your landing page, you might get only 5 or 10 new customers.

That said, if you're spending a good chunk of change on a mobile marketing campaign, you might be driving tens of thousands of people to your mobile landing pages on any given day. For example, if you're a marketer for a nationwide plumbing services company like Roto-Rooter and you're running a mobile paid search campaign using "emergency plumbing service" as your keywords, you might generate 5,000 visits to your website a day. All 5,000 of those people who were driven through to your landing page won't become customers, but 25 or 50 of them will.

Let's say it costs Roto-Rooter 25 cents a click to drive 5,000 customer prospects a day to its mobile website. That means it's costing the company $1,250 per day to run the campaign. If Roto-Rooter's customer lifetime value is $500, and it generates 25 new customers a day from its campaign, then Roto-Rooter is generating $12,500 in CLV each day the campaign runs. As long as the company's COCA is about 10 percent of that figure, then you know it's got an effective mobile marketing campaign.

Step-by-Step Guide to Calculating Your Mobile Marketing ROI

We've covered a lot of concepts over the last few pages, so let's recap by walking through a step-by-step guide on how to calculate the ROI from your mobile marketing campaign.

Step 1: Calculate your CLV. Take your average revenue per customer and multiply it by the number of times your average customer comes back for repeat visits. (For example: $50 per customer × average of 18 visits = $900)

Step 2: Calculate your allowable COCA. Next take your CLV and allocate 10 percent of that figure as your allowable cost of customer acquisition. Some companies may allocate 5 percent, others 15 percent, but a good starting point is 10 percent. (For the example in step 1, you'd take $900 and allocate 10 percent of that, or $90, as your allowable COCA.)

Step 3: Reallocate part of your marketing budget to mobile. Decide what percentage of your overall marketing budget you want to allocate to your mobile marketing campaign. A good idea here is to divide your original marketing budget into two categories: branding and direct response. Your branding budget is a different animal because it's really intended just to create an emotional connection with prospective customers. So take your branding budget and put that aside. Now take your direct response budget—in other words, the budget you use to specifically acquire new customers—and put that in another bucket. Take that figure and slice off 10 or 20 percent for your mobile marketing campaign.

Step 4: Calculate the estimated number of customers you expect to generate from your new mobile marketing campaign. If the direct response budget referenced in step 3 is, say, $500,000 annually, and it generates 5,000 new customers a year for you, then you know your cost of customer acquisition is $100 ($500,000 ÷ 5,000 new customers = $100 per new customer). Take 10 percent of that $500,000 budget (i.e., $50,000) and allocate it to your mobile marketing budget. All things being equal, that $50,000 should generate 500 new customers for you.

Step 5: Create a mobile marketing plan that has tracking mechanisms. Now that you have a $50,000 budget for your mobile marketing campaign, you can start allocating money to various mobile marketing efforts. For our purposes here, you'll want to make sure that 100 percent of your budget is allocated to factors that are trackable. Don't use any of this $50,000 to redesign your mobile website, since that's a *branding* tactic that can't be easily tracked. Instead, use the $50,000 to create 2D code promotions (trackable), SMS/MMS campaigns (trackable), mobile display ads (trackable), mobile paid search ads (trackable), and location-based marketing campaigns (trackable).

Step 6: Launch the campaign and monitor your results. Once you've planned your campaign and confirmed that it's 100 percent trackable, it's time to flip the switch. Be sure to monitor your results closely, and after you've given your campaign a few months to run, don't hesitate to move your dollars away from features that aren't working and toward those that are. As mentioned, after giving the campaign a few months to take effect, you'll want to put on your "media neutral" hat and move your money around to where it can do the most good.

Step 7: Don't expect miracles. This may be your first mobile marketing campaign; and even if it's not, don't expect it to run smoothly the first time around. You'll have campaigns that fail completely, and you'll have others that underperform. But your goal is to determine which campaigns are working, figure out how to replicate what's working in those campaigns, and, finally, apply that knowledge to your other efforts.

In the end, if you set up your mobile marketing campaign so that it's measurable, you'll have much greater success than if you simply throw some tactics on the wall and hope they stick. A little effort and planning in the early stages will go a long way toward producing a campaign that meets your expectations and, more importantly, with the approval of your CEO and CFO.

Do This:

♦ Calculate your customer lifetime value. Even if you're in an industry that makes it difficult to calculate CLV accurately, it's better to have an estimate than to ignore it completely.

♦ Track your results. There's no point running any marketing campaign if you're not going to track its results. One of the best aspects of mobile is that it's digital, and marketing campaigns that are digital are easy to track.

- Use the step-by-step guide. Follow the steps outlined at the end of this chapter to help you set up your mobile marketing campaign. By following these steps, you'll be able to track your results most effectively.

Don't Do This:
- Don't think tactically. A common mistake is for people to get swept up in a new tool (like foursquare) and run a campaign before thinking about it strategically. Before you launch your campaign, be sure you've set objectives, agreed to strategies, and mapped out an executional road map.
- Don't focus exclusively on branding. Any well-run marketing campaign will have a good portion of its budget allocated to branding efforts. But if you're going to track your mobile marketing campaign on an ROI basis, you'll need to focus on highly trackable tools such as 2D code promotions, SMS/MMS campaigns, mobile display ads, mobile paid search ads, and location-based marketing campaigns.

Chapter 21

The 17 Rs of Mobile Marketing and a Step-by-Step Checklist

We've been through a lot together over the course of this book. We've explored the mobile marketing landscape; we've shown you how to set yourself up for success on it; we've investigated the key mobile marketing tools; and we've expanded into other topics, like B2B mobile marketing and mobile e-commerce.

That's a lot to cover, and it can seem confusing and a bit overwhelming. To help ease the confusion, in this chapter we provide two lists that will help you sort things out and keep thing straight.

The Rs of Mobile Marketing

The first list is called the "17 Rs of Mobile Marketing." It comprises 17 important objectives to keep in mind as you manage your mobile marketing campaign.

The 17 Rs of Mobile Marketing

1. *Review* your web analytics and determine what percent of your visitors are using mobile devices to access your website. Tablets, iPads, iPhones, and other smartphones are becoming common devices for accessing the web.
2. *Relevant* messages are a critical part of mobile marketing. If your customers are receiving SMS text messages from your

business that do not foster your relationship with them, they may unsubscribe from your services—or, even worse, stop buying altogether.

3. *Request* feedback from your subscribers; ask how they perceive your mobile marketing campaigns. You can do this through regular e-mail; or send a brief SMS message asking them to visit your website and fill out a feedback survey.

4. *Recruit* customers and prospects who are receptive to your mobile marketing campaigns. You can encourage new subscribers through contests or other types of incentives. Be sure to point out to your customers the added value mobile marketing messages will bring to them.

5. *Registering* for your mobile marketing programs should be easy, but do not underestimate the importance of publishing your privacy statement and describing how you intend to use your subscribers' information.

6. *Rate* the usefulness of your campaigns to your subscribers. Do they provide "insider information" that is released to mobile marketing subscribers before everyone else?

7. *Regional* or location-centric messages can be very valuable to your customers, particularly when they are encouraged to visit a local office or store for a special promotion, or when there is a conference, seminar, or event nearby that would be worthwhile for them to participate in.

8. *Reminders* about time-sensitive information or tasks are another great use of mobile marketing messages—especially when a special deal is approaching its end date.

9. *Respect* the frequency of mobile message use. Too many SMS or MMS messages can cause your subscribers to become unsubscribers. Also, if you send too many messages, your subscribers will begin to disregard them.

10. *Return* important status information if subscribers elect to receive the notification. "Your order has been filled, and here is your tracking number" is one notification that many customers find very helpful.

11. *Respond* to any replied texts as you would any other customer service or marketing inquiry. Text messages are just as important as phone calls or letters.

12. *Record* and document any concerns, complaints, or other feedback; then act on concerns or complaints in a timely manner. Sometimes, this may mean a change in the campaign strategy.

13. *Responsible* campaigns and programs will encourage customers to be on the lookout for the next notification. Design your campaigns to be brief yet tantalizing to your target groups.

14. *Referral* campaigns can be an effective way to gain new subscribers and customers. Encourage your existing customers to spread the word, and offer an incentive to boost their motivation.

15. *Rely* on good systems and software that deploy your mobile marketing messages reliably, and that measure and provide statistics, such as the number of successful receipts and any returned errors.

16. The *reality* is that mobile marketing is new, and therefore not many companies have fully adopted a mobile marketing strategy for their business clients. Also, not all customers want to receive SMS, MMS, or other mobile marketing messages. However, a growing number of users are today relying heavily on mobile devices and so would welcome the opportunity to receive your mobile notices. Have patience; recognize that this is a growing market segment—and the growth rate is definitely accelerating. (Yes, we realize this objective starts with a "T" not an "R," but, hey, nobody is perfect.)

17. *Rapid* adaptation to new trends and techniques in mobile marketing must be incorporated into your plan's strategy. If a mobile campaign is not working, or if there is a better way to implement a program, do not hesitate to change your plans. Keep in mind, mobile users often expect frequent changes, so don't be afraid to institute routine changes and improvements as part of your mobile marketing strategy.

By keeping your customers always in mind and focusing on their ongoing need for responsible communications, you can nurture your business relationships through mobile marketing campaigns that are part of your comprehensive marketing program.

Mobile Marketing Checklist

Now it's time to take a look at the mobile marketing checklist. It is designed as a step-by-step guide to help you set up, launch, and run your campaign.

The checklist is divided into five parts, and we start at square one—reviewing your company's mission, goals, and objective—to ensure that your campaign gets off to the right start.

Ready? Here goes.

Laying the Foundation for Your Campaign

☐ Review your company's business and understand its *mission, goals*, and *objectives*.

☐ Review your company's sales program and understand how prospects are brought into the sales funnel and converted into customers.

☐ Review your company's marketing program and understand what role it plays in the overall success of the company.

☐ Before you move on to the next section, ask yourself, "Is mobile marketing right for my company?" If you conclude that it is, continue with the competitor review.

Competitor Review

☐ Review the strengths and weaknesses of your company's top competitors.

☐ Assess the sales and marketing efforts of your top competitors.

☐ Analyze the specific mobile marketing campaigns being conducted by your top competitors.

☐ Create a list of mobile marketing strategies and tactics that your competitors are using and that appear to be working.

☐ Generate a list of mobile marketing strategies and tactics that your competitors are using and that appear to be failures.

☐ Study both lists. Learn from both.

Setting Yourself Up for Success

☐ Assemble a mobile marketing team to help execute your program. (Your team can be as small as 1 or as large as 100-plus).

☐ Review the Four Ps and Five Cs in Chapter 7. Think through how they apply to your business.

☐ Set S.M.A.R.T. (specific, measurable, actionable, realistic, and time-bound) goals for your mobile marketing campaign.

☐ Review your S.M.A.R.T. goals with your team; encourage their feedback and input.

☐ Conduct an in-depth analysis of your target market to gain a genuine understanding of who they are and what makes them tick.

☐ Define your primary, secondary, and tertiary target markets. Avoid being too specific (e.g., 31-year-old male business-people living in Manhattan) or too vague (e.g., teenagers).

☐ Develop an overall *strategy* for your mobile marketing campaign that will help you accomplish your overall business goals.

☐ Develop a list of *tactics* for your mobile marketing campaign that will help you accomplish your strategic goals.

☐ Develop an *executional timeline* for your mobile marketing program that will help you accomplish your tactical goals.

Budgeting and Scheduling

☐ Establish a launch date for your campaign. Take seasonality into consideration.

☐ Review your budget again. Is there any place you can squeeze 10 percent more efficiency out of your numbers?

☐ What kind of messages do you want to send via your campaign? Branding messages? Direct response messages? Or something in between?

Measuring Your Success

☐ Come to agreement with your team on what your customer lifetime value is.

☐ Establish your allowable cost of customer acquisition.

☐ Run a test campaign before deploying the real thing.

☐ Once you've launched your campaign, run a split test so you can measure the success of each program.

☐ The winner of the split test will be your *control*. Test other campaigns against your control. See if you can beat its results.

☐ Provide regular updates to management on the ROI from your mobile marketing campaign. Refer back to Chapter 20 for specifics on calculating your ROI.

By using this checklist, you should end up with a good, solid foundation for setting up, launching, and running your mobile marketing campaign. To be sure, there are nuances and details that we didn't include on the list, but it should give you a head start in kicking off a successful campaign.

In the next, and final, chapter, we supplement the information in this one with descriptions of the three characteristics of a successful mobile marketing campaign. It's one of the more important chapters, and we've saved it for last to conclude by providing a comprehensive look at what separates an ordinary campaign from a stellar campaign.

Do This:

- ◆ Review the 17 Rs. Keep them in mind as you launch your campaign.
- ◆ Share the mobile marketing checklist in this chapter with the other members of your team.
- ◆ Revisit the checklist as you're setting up, launching, and running your campaign, to keep you on track.

Don't Do This:

- ◆ Don't forget to set up your campaign so it can be tracked and measured.
- ◆ Don't think tactics first; think goals and objectives first, then set up your campaign so you can track your progress toward those goals.

Chapter 22

Three Characteristics of Successful Mobile Marketing Campaigns

We've covered a lot of ground in *Go Mobile*. We've discussed the incredible growth of mobile media. We've explored the different ways consumers connect with mobile, and we've examined each of the tools businesses are using to create effective mobile marketing campaigns.

All this begs the question: What do all successful mobile marketing campaigns have in common? What are the fundamental characteristics that effective mobile marketing campaigns share? What are the techniques these campaigns use that make them different from other, less effective campaigns?

You may be surprised to hear that, given the breadth and depth of the mobile marketing landscape, the number of essential characteristics that successful mobile marketing campaigns have in common can be distilled down to three. Once you strip away the façade of many successful campaigns, what you uncover are these three key characteristics: *measurability*, *consumer insights*, and *innovation*.

Characteristic 1: Measurability

A sure sign that a campaign will fail to reach its full potential is when a marketing director or business owner launches it without setting up a system to track the results.

Many businesses catch wind of a new and emerging trend like mobile marketing and jump into it before mapping out a strategy or developing tracking mechanisms. Typically, they develop a campaign based on a tactical or executional basis. A common refrain goes like this: "Let's dive into foursquare. The CEO just asked me about it, so let's get one running ASAP."

This ready, fire, aim approach to mobile marketing sets people up for failure. No sooner have they launched the campaign on a tactical whim than the CFO walks in and asks for an ROI analysis of it. Since a tactics-and-execution-first approach was taken to set it up, probably very little effort was put into defining tracking mechanisms. The end result is a campaign that flounders because nobody can accurately assess whether it is successful or not.

Successful campaigns start with an agreement about which metrics will be used to track the results. Then a baseline is established; thus, if one of the metrics that will be used is number of clicks to the mobile website, a baseline for that metric needs to be established *prior* to launching the campaign. Here's an example: If a mobile website generates 1,000 visits a week prior to launching a paid search campaign, and it jumps up to 1,250 visits per week following the run of that campaign, then you know it generated a 25 percent increase in visits to the website (assuming all other variables remained the same).

Characteristic 2: Customer Insights

Understandably, it's easy to get swept up in the enthusiasm surrounding a new marketing trend, especially one as exciting as mobile. Consider what happened with social media: Businesspeople were so enthused about its potential that they started to believe it was going to solve all their marketing problems. The thinking was, if we just upload a few YouTube videos and create a Facebook page, we'll be off to the races.

The truth is, it takes more than uploading a few YouTube videos and creating a Facebook page to make a successful social media campaign. Similarly, it takes more than creating a mobile website and running a mobile search program to produce a successful mobile media campaign. It takes careful planning and development, *plus valuable consumer insight.*

Companies that focus on the technology first and the consumer second are destined to fail. Successful mobile marketing campaigns *start* by gaining consumer insight; they then use that insight to grow their sales and revenue. They analyze how their customers and prospects *think and behave*, then try to figure out how mobile marketing can be used to leverage those thoughts and behaviors.

Fandango, the movie ticketing destination, for example, worked to analyze the behavior of people visiting its mobile app. It realized that potential ticket buyers wanted three things: the ability to check movie times, the ability to purchase tickets, and the convenience of not having to stand in line to pick up their tickets when they arrived at the theater. So Fandango created an app that meets those wants: It gives moviegoers the ability to check movie times and purchase tickets, and sends them a QR code they can scan at the ticket booth. By drilling down and analyzing the consumer thought process, Fandango found the way to deliver a superior ticket-buying experience to its customers and, ultimately, improve customer loyalty.

Characteristic 3: Innovation

No doubt you're excited about all the possibilities for business growth offered by mobile marketing. And based on what you've read in this book, you now know that many of your competitors are probably still lagging behind in this trend. So it may be tempting, once you've created your mobile website and perhaps even developed a mobile promotion, to get complacent and comfortable with your accomplishment. That would be a mistake. Successful campaigns typically continue to add an *innovative* element to the mix. They do more than, say, offer a free product sample for people who scan their QR code. Instead, they may engage their consumer in a new and innovative way that leverages the unique characteristics of mobile devices.

■ ■ ■

Now that we've introduced these unique characteristics, let's take a quick look at each of them before we analyze how they're being used in mobile marketing campaigns around the globe. As mentioned, mobile devices have GPS technology that allows users and marketers alike to target prospects based on their locations. And recall that a mobile device's accelerometer can be used to track the speed at which someone is traveling, and even to sense when the mobile device is being shaken. The compass lets marketers find out which direction the user is facing (always helpful for apps like Yelp that provide restaurant ratings to the user based on which direction they're facing).

More, mobile devices have the capability to scan 2D codes, share data and information, and recognize when the mobile device is being held close to a person's body. Mobile devices also can adjust screen brightness based on the ambient light. They also can transfer information wirelessly using NFC or Bluetooth technology.

In a nutshell, the most effective mobile marketing campaigns use these unique characteristics to provide consumers with an experience that's *memorable*. They leverage these attributes in order to connect with consumers more deeply than campaigns that follow traditional, more well-worn paths.

A Few Final Thoughts

If you're reading these words, the odds are you have more than just a passing interest in mobile marketing. You're excited about the prospects this new tool can drive to your business. You might even have some specific ideas for campaigns you're thinking about launching as a result of reading this book.

But there's one last point we need to express to ensure that your mobile marketing campaign will not just work, but succeed. It's the most important point of all—which is why we've saved it for last. That final point is for you to *take action*. Don't just think about, and talk about, mobile marketing. Don't just strategize about it, either. Take action!

We've been tossing around two phrases to each other as we've been writing this book. The first is GSD, which stands for *get stuff done*. (GSD actually stands for something a little edgier than that, but we're too polite to tell you.) The key thrust of GSD is that it motivates people to *take action* instead of just *talking* about taking action. There's a big difference.

The second phrase is: *It's better to get 10 things done than to get 1 thing done perfectly*. Now, we realize that if you're a brain surgeon, this advice does not apply to you. But marketing isn't brain surgery; it's a much more flexible profession. And it happens much more quickly. That means if you don't keep the ball moving forward, the business world will pass you by. Quickly.

So keep those two final points in mind as you take steps to launch your mobile marketing campaign. By doing so, we're confident you'll be able to launch your campaign and still have time to tweak and adjust it while your competitors are stuck in the planning stages.

Good luck. Keep us posted on your results. And let us know what you're doing in the amazing and exciting new world of mobile marketing.

Index

228

Index